simply ®

meditation

simply ®

meditation

LYNNE LAUREN

STERLING/ZAMBEZI
An imprint of Sterling Publishing Co., Inc.

New York / London
www.sterlingpublishing.com

STERLING and the distinctive Sterling logo are registered trademarks of Sterling Publishing Co., Inc.

Library of Congress Cataloging-in-Publication Data
Lauren, Lynne.
Simply meditation / Lynne Lauren.
p. cm.
Includes index.
ISBN 978-1-4027-5456-2
1. Meditation—Therapeutic use. I. Title.
RC489.M43L38 2009
615.8'52—dc22
2009014797

2   4   6   8   10   9   7   5   3   1

Published by Sterling Publishing Co., Inc.
387 Park Avenue South, New York, NY 10016
Text © 2010 by Lynne Lauren
Illustrations © 2010 Adam Reiti
Distributed in Canada by Sterling Publishing
c/o Canadian Manda Group, 165 Dufferin Street
Toronto, Ontario, Canada M6K 3H6
Published in the UK solely by Zambezi Publishing Ltd.
P.O. Box 221, Plymouth, PL2 2EQ
Distributed in Australia by Capricorn Link (Australia) Pty. Ltd.
P.O. Box 704, Windsor, NSW 2756, Australia

Sterling ISBN 978-1-4027-5456-2
Zambezi ISBN 978-1-903065-65-5

For information about custom editions, special sales, premium and corporate purchases, please contact Sterling Special Sales Department at 800-805-5489 or specialsales@sterlingpublishing.com.

To my beautiful girls,

Kaeleigh and Stevie,

and all our children of tomorrow

contents

introduction

Meditation is a practice that calms the mind and body in a natural way. Its aim is to quiet or still the mind; this leads to calm awareness, without the interference of troublesome thoughts.

You can practice meditation at your own pace in your own time, however; no matter how infrequently you do so, it will still have a beneficial effect, and the more you practice, the easier it becomes.

Although meditation is relaxing, it should not be mistaken for a method of relaxation, because you must relax first in order to meditate. You don't put yourself into a sleepy daydream or faraway state of mind, and you do not simply make your mind a blank. Meditation is a way of clearing your mind and controlling your thoughts and emotions so you are functioning as your true self. You are not in a hypnotic state; you are fully aware of what is happening in the here and now. Normally in life we put a lot of energy into thinking up ways of doing things or of achieving our goals, but as we begin to practice meditation, we break free and behave in the opposite way. Our energy is focused not on *doing* but on *being*, on ourselves, and on getting back to our real selves, our true nature.

Meditation techniques can range from chants, gentle breathing exercises, and emptying the mind to focus on one topic (single-point meditation), one movement, or one of the five senses, to deep contemplation. In the East, meditation is a central part of several religions and has been practiced for more than five thousand years to promote tranquility, awareness, and wisdom. Some of these methods are incorporated in the following practices.

BUDDHIST MEDITATION

Buddhist meditation involves a variety of techniques, including breath control and focusing on one's mind (being aware of one's thoughts, one's actions, and the here and now). Another meditation technique centers on visualizations, or putting pictures in your mind, in other words, "seeing" a place, person, or situation in your mind's eye. These techniques are designed to develop the mind, improve concentration, and provide insight, peace, and tranquility.

TAOIST MEDITATION

Taoist meditation has no religious background but is a way of being that works through meditation. The body is regarded as sacred and is used to charge the body's natural energy into a force known as chi. This energy is then circulated internally. When the chi is flowing in your body and in the environment, you feel balanced with your true self, calmed, and energized. Once an individual finds his or her chi, the chi can be focused toward improvement of the self or toward attaining goals in life. It is believed that once an individual finds his or her chi, the individual need put very little effort into life because it falls into place easily.

TRANSCENDENTAL MEDITATION

Maharishi Mahesh Yogi founded Transcendental Meditation, a mantra-based form of meditation, in 1958. Mantras are words, phrases, or sentences that when repeated have a power and energy that can have a positive effect on the person who says them. Essentially, this practice involves sitting with closed eyes, twice a day for fifteen or twenty minutes at a time, while mentally repeating a mantra. The long-term aims are to move beyond the first three major states of consciousness— waking, dreaming, and deep, dreamless sleep—into the fourth state, the state of transcendental consciousness. With this technique your body and mind can gain deep relief from both mental and physical stress.

ZEN MEDITATION

Zen meditation is a form of Buddhist meditation that simply means "seated meditation." A type of Zen meditation is *Zazen*, which means "just sitting." This form of practice is highly personal; it is designed so that you seek enlightenment by focusing on the question, "What is life?" It also includes other forms of meditation such as stilling the mind, which stops the person from thinking about day-to-day problems for a while. This involves the use of koans, which are stories, questions, or statements that go beyond rational under-standing and activate the intuition. For instance, if you clap using two hands, there is a sound, but what sound is made if only one hand claps?

WHY MEDITATE?

Meditation can help you to focus, de-stress, lift a low mood, heal, let go, improve your intuition, and keep your life in balance. It's the only way of feeling permanently calm and tranquil that has been available to us up until now. Other ways of calming, such as drugs and alcohol, produce only a temporary escape and relief.

Who you are and how your life flows begin with your mind. You create your world, and your mind is the workshop where it all begins. You choose who you want to be, who is in your life, and how you deal with them. You choose what work you do, where you live, how you present yourself. You are the real person in control in your life, and others cannot really make you do anything unless you agree to let them. When you are really happy, you do not think and your mind is calm. If you feel you aren't good enough or that good things will never come to you, then they never will, because you will never allow them to. Fears and phobias, or ideas such as believing that you can't live without something or that what you want is always going to be out of your reach, are the inventions of your own mind. In reality there is little outside of you that is stopping you from living as you want to and being who you really want to be. Meditation is a way of working on the mind in an unfolding and gentle manner, allowing you to realize, understand, and undo whatever is restricting you or making you unhappy. It also allows you to get to know your real self and to make changes that can help you communicate and handle life more easily. It can help you deal with and rise above the pressures of everyday living.

1

ABOUT MEDITATION

WHERE TO MEDITATE

As you practice meditation, you will find that you can do many of the simple exercises in a few minutes, anywhere and anytime. You will get better at distancing yourself from your surroundings and focusing inwardly. The more you can bring meditation into your daily life, the more positive results you will see and the calmer you will feel.

If you plan to meditate often or as a regular part of your routine, you'll find it useful to choose a quiet space with few distractions, where you feel happy and where you can sit comfortably. It is especially good for your progress if the space you allocate is used *only* for meditation, as the space will accumulate a good vibration and will become associated with the benefits of meditation. Good places include an area of your bedroom or a living room. Keeping the meditation area simple will help prevent distractions. You will find it

calming if the walls or surroundings are pastel colors such as lilac, blue, or green or neutral colors such as cream or white. In the summer you may feel like using a corner of the garden or perhaps a summerhouse, sunroom, or conservatory. This is especially good if you want to focus on natural objects, such as plants or trees.

You will need something comfortable to sit on. An ordinary comfortable chair is fine; you may also use a hard high-backed chair with a cushion if you need to support your back. If you want to meditate in true Eastern style, sit cross-legged on a cushion.

Your posture is important, especially when practicing Buddhist, Zen, and Tao meditations, as these are longer meditations. It is important to keep your back straight so that you stay comfortable. If you imagine that there is an invisible thread pulling up the top of your head and straightening your back, this can be a comfortable posture to maintain while doing any seated meditation. Your clothing should be comfortable and nonrestricting. Should you prefer to use incense, it is a good idea to use a stick that will last roughly the length of your meditation.

Meditate at the time of day that suits you best—for instance, during the morning, if that's when your mind is fresh. If you wake in the early hours and find you can't get back to sleep, this is also a good time, as meditation can focus and calm you. By setting a regular time slot for meditation, you will soon find that you look forward to it as a change from the normal stress-engaging activities.

THE MEDITATIONS IN THIS BOOK

Many of the meditations in this book are quick and effective, and you can even do some of them as you go about your daily life, say, while traveling on a train or bus or while waiting in line. (Never meditate while driving, though.) If you are sitting and worrying about something, try a meditation; you may find that it helps to relieve your worry.

Many of the meditations in this book are based on the technique of visualization, in other words, creating pictures or images in your mind. You will "see" the person or problem with your mind's eye, and then use further images or pictures to solve or heal the problem. Think of it as using your imagination to direct your own inner movie.

Visualizing in meditation works effectively on three aspects of our makeup: our physical bodies, our emotions, and our spiritual or soul level. Your body will believe the images that your mind focuses on, and here's why: your mind uses the images that your physical eyes see to enable you to live, so it will accept the images that your inner eye shows it, and then your mind will tell your body how to act. Just as your mind can tell you how to sit in a chair by gauging it's shape and size, so your mind can work on the healing of an organ in your body if you can see it becoming healed. Believe, and your body will respond.

The emotions are linked to the creative sides of the brain, so they respond to music, poetry, art, and images. If you picture a beautiful deserted island scene, you will feel your emotions reacting. When you are developing your psychic or spiritual skills, your imagination will trigger your third eye, the center that controls your psychic senses. For instance, if you look back into your past and the things that influenced you in your early days, you often can recall experiences as feelings or pictures. We all have childhood memories, usually in the form of images in the part of our mind that still connects us to our childhood or our inner child.

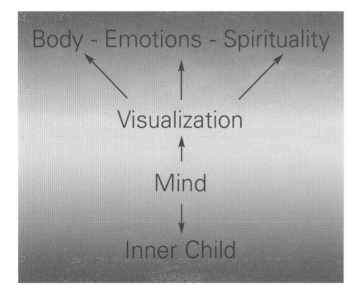

Our minds have been shaped by our childhood memories and experiences, but when we are adults, our minds take in information from our eyes, which are our window to the world around us.

ABOUT MEDITATIONS

Many of the meditations in this book have short preparations or exercises that help you to become calm and to focus your mind for the main meditation. These preparatory exercises are called the Key Meditations. You may also find Key Meditation 1 a useful grounding exercise when you need to quiet your mind. It is also a good preparation to do before any meditation, as it will help still your mind. Moreover, it is a complete meditation in itself that you can use anywhere to help calm and focus your mind if you are stressed.

Key Meditation 2 is a longer exercise that is used as a preparation for many psychic and spiritual meditations. It is good for clearing out any "heaviness" you may feel in your body, as heaviness is associated with darkness. Worry and distress can make us feel physically heavy. Key Meditation 2 cleanses and relaxes your body and also lifts your mood, allowing you to feel lighter and happier.

From this framework, you can move toward deeper meditation and spiritual access.

Many meditations require the use of imagination, and this helps the development of your "third eye," which, in turn,

helps improve your intuitive or psychic abilities. The third eye
is also known as the brow chakra; it is located in the middle
of the forehead between and a little above the eyes. You
need to be able to open it in preparation for any kind of psychic or spiritual activity.

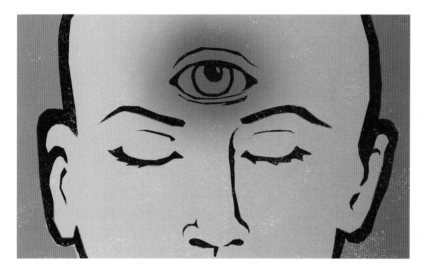

Read through a meditation before following it. You may find
it useful to record some of the longer meditations on tape or
CD, as this makes it easier to do the meditations than if you
had to keep referring back to the book.

2

KEY MEDITATIONS

With these simple visualizations as starting points, you can follow any of the meditations in this book more effectively, as they will allow your focus to be sharper and can make the outcome stronger.

KEY MEDITATION 1: THE "GROUNDING" MEDITATION

You can do the "Grounding" meditation either standing or sitting. It is good for calming and bringing your focus into the present moment, the here and now. It is good for stress if your thoughts are whirling, or if you have just come away from an upsetting occurrence and your mind will not clear.

1. Relax and lower or close your eyes.
2. Focus on the arches of your feet.
3. Visualize two roots, one from each foot, growing down into the ground.
4. Allow the roots to work their way down, deeper and deeper.
5. Let the roots branch out as they go down.
6. Feel yourself becoming calmer the deeper you take your roots.
7. Visualize your roots working their way farther downward.
8. See the roots passing through different layers of soil, clay, and rock.
9. Continue in this way until your feet begin to feel heavy.

10. Then bring your focus back up to your feet.
11. Lift or open your eyes.

Note: If you feel that you are not grounded enough, you can add this second step before opening your eyes.

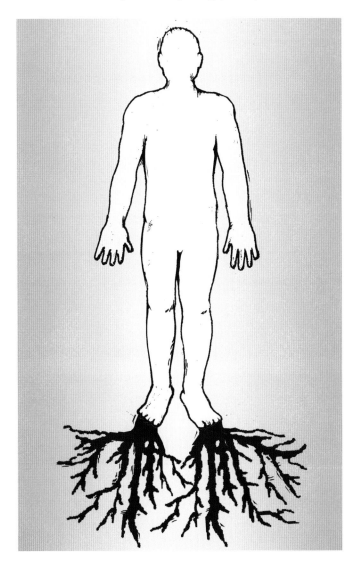

Second Step

1. Take your focus to the base of your spine.
2. Imagine a thick root growing from the base of your spine.
3. See the root growing down through the chair (if you are sitting), then through the floor, and then down into the ground.
4. Watch the root burrowing deeper and deeper.
5. Imagine it branching out into the earth.
6. See it working down through layers of soil, rock, and clay.
7. Feel your back firmly anchored to the chair.
8. Now bring your focus up to the base of your spine.
9. Lift or open your eyes.

KEY MEDITATION 2: THE "WHITE LIGHT" MEDITATION

The "White Light" meditation is a good preparation for any psychic or spiritual meditation and also is an instant mood lightener. If we keep worrying about something, we can store this negative energy in certain parts of our bodies. This can make our bodies feel heavy, and eventually it can make us ill. When we are happy, our bodies feel light. This meditation cleanses you of old suppressed hurts, anxieties, and upsets.

1. Sit quietly, relax, and close your eyes.
2. Take a few deep breaths, keeping your eyes closed.

3. Take your focus to the top of your head.

4. Send up a thought asking for a shaft of white light to come down from the heavens.

5. Visualize the light entering the crown of your head.

6. See the light flowing down into the top of your head, filling your crown.

7. Feel it flowing down into your forehead, eyes, and temples.

8. Let it fill your cheekbones and ears, mouth, chin, and jawbone.

9. See the light completely filling the back and the front of your head.

10. Imagine the light flowing down the length of your neck.

11. Picture it flowing along the top of each shoulder.

12. Let it course down into both arms, right to the fingertips.

13. Now take the light down through your chest and abdomen.

14. Feel the light flowing down both legs and into your feet.

15. When you are completely full of white light, drop the light down through your feet, through the roots, and into the earth.

Working with white light has a threefold advantage. First, it lifts your vibration or the speed of your natural energy, which then lifts and brightens your mood and allows you to meditate more effectively. Second, it helps clear your system of negative energy that has gathered there from tension, stress, or emotional distress. Third, white light opens a clear communication channel that enables guides and the spirit world to contact you quickly and easily.

KEY MEDITATION 3: THE "SPINNING DISC" MEDITATION

The "Spinning Disc" meditation forms the framework for the work you will do on the mental, emotional, and spiritual aspects of yourself.

1. Find a quiet place where you will not be disturbed.
2. Relax, close your eyes, and take a few deep breaths.
3. Take your focus to your third eye, and visualize a white spinning disc.
4. As you watch the disc, see it grow larger and larger.
5. When it is large enough to step through, go through the center.
6. Visualize yourself on an outdoor path on a bright, sunny day.
7. See the path leading you into a lovely garden.
8. Focus on the path meandering ahead.
9. Let it lead you to the front door of a lovely house, your house.
10. Enter the house and close the front door behind you.

11. Go in to the beautiful hallway.

12. In front of you is a large stairway; begin to climb it.

13. Stop on the first landing where there is a large window.

14. Observe it casting pools of sunlight on the floor where you are standing.

15. Notice another stairway descending to a lower floor; go down that.

16. See two corridors leading off to the left and right.

The meditations that use this Key Meditation as preparation continue from this point by directing you to certain parts of the house. The left-hand corridor is used for emotional meditations, and the right-hand one is used for mental meditations, while the stairway going up is used for spiritual-development meditations. The stairway down takes you into deeper strengthening meditations.

3

SPECIFIC MEDITATIONS

The following meditations are designed to clear negative vibes or unpleasant emotions that may linger after encounters with unpleasant people.

CLEARING OUR SYSTEMS OF STRESS

We suffer tension and stress on a daily basis, and unless we unwind properly and let these stressors go, they can build up in our systems, affecting our moods, making us lethargic, and making our bodies feel heavy.

We absorb large amounts of negative vibrations from the world of gadgets (computers, televisions, microwave ovens, telephones, and other contraptions) we live in, and these can also affect our physical and mental states. The moods and actions of other people and our own negative reactions and worries also filter into our systems and can be compounded as we play them over and over in our minds. Eating junk food or processed food that has very little natural goodness in it can upset our bodies, causing us to be fatigued and often irritable. A daily clearing of the general negative energy in our systems helps rid our systems of sluggish energy, calms our moods, and can be enormously energizing. Here are some simple meditations that can be worked into your daily routine. They are quick, and they will drain away any negative energy that you have. You can practice these while sitting at your desk, standing at a bus stop, waiting in line, or even traveling (though of course not while you're driving).

This meditation for clearing stress can be done literally anywhere, even in company. It requires little focus and no visualization. You can effectively use it in the middle of an interview or a meeting or in any situation in which you have to deal with people. It is also useful if you find you are unable to unwind at the end of the day or if you are having trouble sleeping. This meditation is best practiced while sitting.

1. On both hands, touch the ends of your thumbs with your index fingers.
2. Spread wide the other three fingers on both hands.
3. Rest the backs of your hands on your upper thighs.
4. Focus on your breathing and be aware of it becoming calmer.
5. Leave your hands in this position for as long as you need or want.
6. When you finish and release your fingers, allow your breathing to return to normal.

This meditation helps you to slow down your breathing, which in turn helps you to begin to de-stress your nervous system and calm your mind.

TWO MEDITATIONS TO CLEAR YOU OF NEGATIVE ENERGIES

These two meditations can help you draw away hurts, tensions, or upsets that have accumulated in the form of negative energy—energy that may have caused aches and pains—and they can help you feel noticeably lighter afterward. The first meditation can be done standing or sitting, anywhere, at any time of the day; all you need is a minute or two of uninterrupted time. If you feel inclined, you can remove your shoes, as this allows your energy field to expand (the meditation will still work if you don't).

Opening Your Taps or Spouts

1. Relax, take a few deep breaths, and close your eyes.
2. Put your feet flat on the floor.
3. Visualize your body from your feet to the top of your head, and in your mind's eye, see your body becoming pure white.
4. Look down at your feet.
5. Notice any dark negative energy that has risen in your body.
6. Visualize the energy; is it ankle high, thigh high, waist high, or higher?
7. Picture two small camera shutters, one in the sole of each foot.
8. Open the shutters to reveal two small drains, taps, or spouts, one on each foot.
9. Push the negative energy out through these drains.
10. When all the negative energy has gone, close the shutters.
11. Open your eyes.

Washing Your Baggage Away

You may have noticed that you feel lighter or energized after a bath or shower.

Negative energy in the form of anger or aggression can accumulate in the body's energy field or aura. This energy field is made up mainly of the energy we give out; it surrounds our bodies and can extend up to several feet. When you are in water, your aura retracts into your body so that any negative energy in it just drops off.

This meditation is good to do in the bath or shower. It is a quick inner-cleansing and rejuvenating exercise that works while the water is cleansing your energy on the outside!

1. Close your eyes and visualize a white shaft of light.
2. See yourself bringing the light down through the crown of your head.
3. Allow the light to flow down through the inside of your body.
4. See the light washing away dark, negative areas of old negative feelings and tensions.
5. Allow the light to wash the dark energy down toward your feet.
6. Visualize two camera shutters opening, one in the sole of each foot.
7. See the negative energy draining out of your feet and down the drain.
8. Close the two camera shutters.
9. Open your eyes.

THE SIEVE

This meditation is good for when you're feeling over-whelmed with troubles and becoming despondent. It works by clearing your energy field around your body (the aura) as well as your energy system within your body.

1. Take a few deep, long breaths and close your eyes.
2. Under your feet imagine a circular sieve with a fine golden mesh.
3. Envision the sieve extending out around your body.
4. Pull the sieve steadily up from the ground.
5. Focus on the sieve moving steadily up through your body and energy field.
6. Notice it catching and taking any negative energy up with it.
7. Let it move up your whole body and through your head.
8. Let the sieve come to a halt when it clears the top of your head.
9. Now imagine the outer edge of the sieve shrinking like elastic and pulling together so the sieve forms a bag.
10. Take the bag, hold it out a window, and drop it and the negative energy it holds onto the ground.
11. Alternatively, watch the bag float upward until it and the negative energy it contains disappear into the distance.
12. Open your eyes.

If you find that a room or even a whole building has a stale atmosphere, you can "sieve" the room or the building by visualizing the sieve moving upward through the room or building to the top and then picturing the bag floating upward into the distance until it disappears.

SIEVING ON THE INSIDE

This meditation is good to use after an upset.

1. Relax, take a few deep breaths, and close your eyes.
2. Visualize a golden sieve just below the base of your spine.
3. Imagine that it is the same width and depth as your body.
4. Now visualize it moving up under your spine *inside* your body.
5. Move the sieve upward, catching the heavy area.
6. Pull the edges of the sieve together around the heavy energy.
7. Tug the sieve up through your body.
8. Take it out through the crown of your head.
9. Send the sieve out of the window and down into the ground.
10. Alternatively, send the sieve upward until it is a distant speck and diminishes until it disappears.
11. When you are ready, open your eyes.

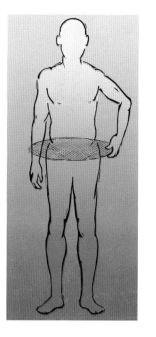

4

CLEARING PAST HURTS

Living in the past and replaying old hurts can hold you back, preventing you from achieving what you want in life or from being the person you want to be. You can get stuck in a rut and become depressed, as your feelings, thoughts, and body absorb the impact of the long-term anger or upset.

Everybody has bad experiences and disappointments in life, and letting go of bad memories or old issues is very important for your health, your confidence, your motivation, the way you function in the world, and the way you deal with other people. If you are holding on to an old hurt, it can prove to be very damaging, not only mentally and emotionally but also physically and spiritually.

BLOCKS

This meditation can take ten to fifteen minutes or longer, so it is best to record it beforehand, and then let the recording guide you.

1. Find a quiet place where you will not be disturbed.
2. Relax, close your eyes, and take a few deep breaths.
3. Take your focus to your third eye and visualize a white spinning disc.
4. Visualize the disc growing larger and larger.
5. Step through the center of the disc and find yourself on a path on a bright, sunny day.

6. Let the path lead you through a lovely garden.

7. Visualize the plants and trees in detail.

8. Imagine that you come across a spiral stairway, descending to a lower level.

9. Count yourself down the ten steps of the staircase.

10. Now find yourself on a lighter path, your time path. It stretches both in front of and behind you. In front of you, picture the path stretching forward and disappearing into a distant horizon.

11. Stand and look forward, with your past behind you.

12. If you feel your past is creeping around the sides or pulling you back, push it firmly behind you, then walk forward, away from it.

13. As you look forward, check to see whether there are obstacles or people hindering your way.
14. If there are, remove them or let them fade away.
15. Alternatively, put them to the side of the path or place them behind you until you can visualize that your path is clear.
16. Now climb back up the ten steps.
17. Make your way through the garden.
18. Step back into the light of your third eye.
19. Blend back in with your body.
20. Align with your body.
21. Wiggle your fingers and toes.
22. When you are ready, open your eyes.

CLEARING RELATIONSHIPS

Sometimes we want to break away from a hurtful relationship but find that we can't let go or that we keep being pulled back. Long after a separation or divorce, a former partner can affect our feelings by upsetting us or by controlling us in some way. We can also feel affected if we allow a destructive friendship to continue when we really should bring it to an end.

The distress or anger you have felt with a person can accumulate and form cords of energy that stretch from that person's heart to yours. The same effect can occur from another person's throat to yours if you have exchanged hurtful words. A cord of energy can link you with another at the center of the abdomen if you have engaged in a power struggle. Former partners tend to be attached to each other at the center of the abdomen or from third eye to third eye. A parent or teacher or anyone who has influenced you can be linked to you with a cord of energy that extends between the crowns of your heads or from the crown of that person's head to the base of your spine.

If you have an uneasy feeling when you think of someone, there is usually a negative cord of energy connecting you. Cutting these cords of negative energy will not harm anything good between you, nor does it dispel these people from your life—unless their reason for being in your life is purely negative. It removes negative influences that are still at work, such as bad thoughts or feelings left over from an argument, from bullying, or from a constant pattern of negative behavior such as lying.

This simple meditation of cutting negative connections can free you to make the changes you need or can help you clear the air and sort things out positively.

Burning Negative Cords

This meditation can be quite effective when it is the last thing you do at night before you go to sleep, because your third eye is very receptive to images at this time. You can also try it if you wake in the night and find yourself thinking of a person in a way that troubles you. After completing this meditation, you may notice a marked difference in what you feel or experience when you see that person again.

1. Take a few deep breaths and close your eyes.
2. Visualize the person standing full length in front of you.
3. Check for cords connecting you to each other that run from the person's center to your center. There may be only one or there may be many.
4. Visualize a colored flame. Beginning with the lowest cord, place the flame at your end of the cord.
5. Allow the flame to burn along the length of the cord.
6. Finish when the flame reaches the other person's center.
7. Leave no ends hanging.
8. Extinguish the flame and begin to work on the next cord; you can use the same color or choose a different one.
9. Keep going until all the cords are burned away.
10. Allow the person to leave your mind's eye.
11. When you are ready, open your eyes.

You may need to repeat this meditation two or three times before you see or feel a difference in your relationship.

Removing Ties

This meditation can be very effective if you have had relationships where the responsibility has been loaded onto you. Maybe you were the one holding the household side together, being the breadwinner and paying the bills. Or you may have been emotionally supportive, providing companionship or keeping someone calm and protected from upsetting situations. You may have coped with someone with an addiction, a depression, or an illness, and that person may have come to expect that you would continue to support him or her whether you wanted to or not.

This meditation can help clear previous patterns of thoughts in which a person expected you to be "doing" for them in some way.

1. Close your eyes and take your focus to your third eye.
2. Envision the person in question standing behind you.
3. Scan for cords connecting you to the other person that are penetrating your back and shoulders.
4. Visualize a colored flame of your choice and begin burning the cords all at the same time, starting at the end that attaches to your body.
5. Picture the flame working back and burning all the cords to their starting points on the other person.

Note: Any color can be used for the flame—red, blue, green, white, whatever—choose the one that is most effective for you.

Freeing Yourself

You are a living being, and life creates energy, and all around your body there is an energy field called your *aura*. A special camera called a Kirlian camera can pick up this energy, and some people can see an aura with their physical eyes or with their inner eye, or third eye. This energy can extend several feet from a person's body. Thoughts and feelings can show up as colors in your aura, so your aura can change from day to day or week to week.

Certain negative energies, such as envy, jealousy, resentment, impatience, and anger, can be directed toward you from people you know or have known, and even from those whom you have only briefly met. You may have felt this energy, or you may have been upset by it afterward if you absorbed it. It will have formed a restrictive layer around you, and it can show up as a dark area in your aura. This can make you feel vulnerable, fearful, or anxious.

If people have thought badly of you, whether you feel you have deserved it or not, or if you keep attracting negative reactions from others, try the next meditation. If there is a negative band of energy around you, when you remove it you will feel a rush of fresh energy flow from the base of your spine upward at the end of the meditation.

With some practice you will find that you can do this meditation anywhere and at any time in the space of a few moments.

1. Relax, lower or close your eyes, and take a few deep breaths.
2. Visualize the person in question standing full length in front of you.
3. Scan your head to see whether a dark cap (like an old rubber bathing cap) is on your head.

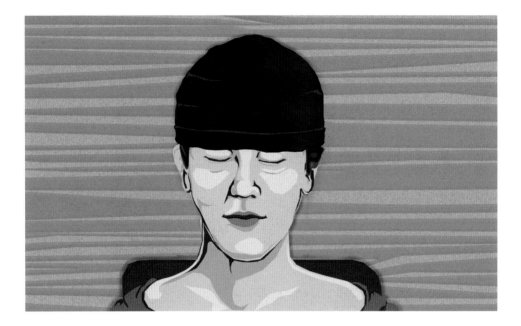

4. Check to see how far it has stretched down your body. It may cover your head, come down to your shoulders, and stretch over your chest; it may even cover your whole body.

5. Grab the ends of the cap and roll it back up until you can lift it off your head.

6. Send it out of the window and drop it to the ground outside.

7. When you feel ready, open your eyes.

5

CHANGING YOUR WORLD

This section helps you focus on those parts of your nature that you dislike. If you need to improve your self-esteem, these affirmations will do a lot to help.

There can be many reasons that people feel that they are unable to cope with life. For instance, some may feel they aren't strong enough to stand up to difficult people at work or at home, and situations might pile on the stress when you are least able to handle it. If you feel inadequate for any reason, a positive affirmation can help you become stronger.

Alternatively, you might want to focus on working on your own emotions, especially negative ones, such as anger or jealousy. If you feel that your emotions are out of kilter, the meditations, grounding techniques, and affirmations in this chapter can help. Even if you feel reasonably happy about yourself but still want to bring some part of your mind or body into balance, the following meditations, grounding methods, and affirmations may be useful.

Included in each section are affirmations. These are positive words or statements that build and confirm good things about you. Examples include "I am strong" or "Who I am is good." When you repeat these meditations, they can help guide and strengthen you into thinking positively about yourself. It is important to say each affirmation at least three times to allow it to sink in and take effect. For an even greater effect, repeat each affirmation three times, and then do another two sets of three.

It's best to repeat your affirmations in sets of three over a period of at least a few days, and preferably a few weeks, to feel their full benefit. With affirmations, if you are using a phrase or sentence, you must say it in a way that indicates that it is *already happening* ("I am strong") not that it *will happen* ("I will be strong"), as that suggests some time in the future, and your affirmations are intended to reinforce your positive feelings about yourself in the here and now.

SECURITY

We all have an innate desire to live and survive on this planet. We have a natural instinct to provide ourselves with food, warmth, and shelter. We also have a built-in sense of danger and a basic sense of what we believe to be right or wrong.

When Balanced

- You feel confident about generating enough money and handling it properly, you feel that you're in the right job, and you feel safe in your home.
- You feel happy about life.
- You are as content in your own company as in the company of others.

When Out of Balance

- You can feel lonely.
- You can have an unfocused mind or feel spaced-out or out of touch with things.

- You can be greedy or stingy about money or possessions.
- You have difficulty caring for yourself and want others to look after you.
- You find it hard to cope with everyday life and achieving the basic things you need.

Affirmations

- I am strong and independent.
- I manage life easily.
- I always have what I need.
- Life becomes better and easier each day.

Say these affirmations, and then, wherever you are, stop and listen to the sound of your breathing. Now listen to the sounds around you. Keep listening until you have heard and counted five different sounds.

If you feel that you have lost your way in life or that some part of your personality is out of balance, try the following meditations.

Grounding

Follow Key Meditation 1: The "Grounding" meditation, and add the following steps:

- Send a thick taproot down to the Earth from the base of your spine.
- Anchor this root in rock.
- Bring your focus back up.

- Center your focus just below your breastbone.
- Lift or open your eyes.

A MEDITATION THAT BRINGS A RENEWAL OF ENERGY

This meditation can help you to feel part of the world and the human race again, and it can activate your ability to get the basics of life together. Rather than visualizing anything in detail, it is better for you to focus on feeling that you are alive, here, and happy. For this meditation you need ten to fifteen minutes of quiet privacy.

Connect Yourself Back to Life

1. Find a quiet place, sit and relax, and close or lower your eyes.
2. Take your focus to your third eye.
3. Visualize the color indigo.
4. Now see the color clearing.
5. Visualize yourself on a precipice looking at the Earth from a distance.
6. Watch the planet as it begins to move closer to you. It approaches, growing larger and larger. Soon it is very close.
7. See a white bridge forming that connects the precipice to the Earth.
8. Set off across the bridge.
9. Let it take you through gentle clouds.

10. Picture in front of you a white wall with climbing plants growing up it.

11. There is an opening in the wall; let the bridge take you through it. There is a gentle mist around you that fades and clears.

12. Notice your surroundings: around you natural branches are wound together. You are in a tree house not far from the ground. The branches wind around the sides and roof. The floor is made up of soft, warm moss. There is a doorway and a short ladder to the ground.

13. Stay here until you are ready to climb down the ladder.
14. When you feel it is time to do so, climb down.
15. When your bare feet have touched the ground, feel the creative Earth energy drawing up into your feet.
16. Take a walk through the countryside of your choice.
17. Then return to your home.
18. When you are ready, open your eyes.

TRUSTING

When you mistrust others, you harbor underlying feelings of mistrust for yourself. We all come into this life trusting ourselves and knowing who is good for us and who is not, but we have also learned how to see ourselves and how to react to situations as a result of programming by our parents or family, and sometimes this is not how we would naturally be. We need to believe and trust who we naturally are. We need to relearn how to trust our own instincts.

When Balanced

- You have self-control.
- You feel able to handle tricky situations positively and successfully.
- You are able to stand up for yourself when you feel you are right.
- You believe in what you do and what you say.

When Out of Balance

- You distrust the world or feel everyone rejects you.
- You don't trust your feelings, and, therefore, you don't feel in control of your life.
- You don't trust yourself to do the right thing.
- If you doubt or dislike yourself, you may act like the victim or even display a cruel streak.
- You allow others to dominate you, as you don't have a will of your own.

Affirmations

- Who I am is good.
- I am in charge of my life.
- I always take care of me.
- My decisions are good.

Admit Your Feelings

You can use the following meditation for looking into one feeling or for checking out a collection of emotions. It will help you uncover what you really think or feel, as opposed to what you have been taught to think and feel.

1. Sit quietly and close your eyes.
2. Allow a situation to run through your mind.
3. Focus on what you feel.
4. Admit to yourself what you feel.
5. Give yourself permission to have these feelings.
6. Now drain the feelings down your body.

7. Take them out through your feet.
8. Review a situation that concerns you.
9. Ask yourself what you want to happen.
10. When you feel you have an answer, open
    your eyes.

When you want to blame someone else or feel you cannot cope with a situation, try this short meditation.

1. Relax and take a few deep breaths.
2. See a stranger in your situation.
3. Listen as the stranger tells you what is wrong.
4. Advise the stranger; tell this person what he or she needs to do to fix what is wrong.
5. Find out whether the person needs input from another source, for instance, another person, a professional body, or some other resource.
6. Determine what alternative methods are available to fix the problem.
7. Visualize the stranger feeling strong and on top of the world while he or she addresses and fixes the problem.
8. Now apply this same meditation to yourself.

STORED EMOTIONS

We store our earliest feelings deep within us, and they influence the way we handle relationships and show our feelings. Whether we tend to feel rejected or accepted by others will shape our relationships and sexuality. Our emotions are important because our creative ideas spring from them and they also show us what we want and allow us to feel that we belong in the world.

When Balanced

- Your emotions are genuine, honest, expressive, and giving.
- Your emotions are neither over-the-top nor gushing.
- You express emotional and sexual needs naturally and don't overpower others with them.

When Out of Balance

- You are confused about what you feel, and you don't trust your feelings.
- You suffer unnecessary guilt or self-disapproval.
- You feel sorry for yourself or play the martyr.
- You hold distress or anger inside for long periods and then explode.
- You criticize yourself a lot.
- You can be oversensitive if you have lost someone close.

Affirmations

- I listen to my feelings.
- I trust what I feel.
- I love and accept love easily.

- I am happy sharing with my partner.
- I love my sexuality.
- I know my feelings and I know myself.

Admit What You Feel

1. Find a quiet place and sit.
2. Complete Key Meditation 1: The "Grounding" Meditation.
3. Focus on what is upsetting you.
4. Look at your feelings right now without deciding whether they are right or wrong.
5. Simply admit that you feel your emotions and that it is all right to feel them.
6. Now sit quietly for a moment until you feel ready to open your eyes and get back to your normal busy life once again.

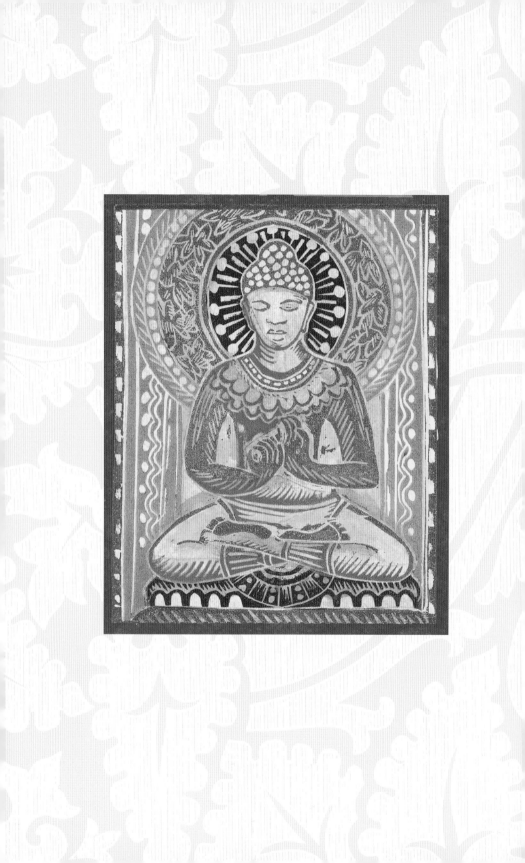

HEALING YOUR EMOTIONS

This meditation is useful if you have suffered from the breakup of a relationship. Use it if a partner has left you, if your partner has been deceitful, or if you have suffered rejection from someone you love, including friends or family.

1. Find a quiet space and sit with your eyes closed.
2. Imagine a white spinning light in the center of your forehead.
3. Enlarge the light and step through it.
4. Now see yourself in a clean, white artist's studio.
5. Set a large white canvas in front of you.

6. Visualize a hurtful situation that is bothering you.
7. Freeze-frame the situation at what you perceive to be the worst point.
8. Paint in the person who has hurt you.
9. Paint in the surroundings you were in.
10. Paint in any other people involved, excluding you.

11. Drain the color out of the painting, turning all the images to black and white.
12. Shrink your painting of the situation down to a small square in the center of the canvas.
13. Load a paintbrush with white paint.
14. Paint out the picture completely.
15. Open your eyes.

If you have had a series of upsetting events, paint the first event and shrink it, as instructed in the meditation, and then place it at the top left-hand side of the canvas. Paint and shrink the next event, and line it up next to the first one. Continue in this manner for any additional events, lining each one up so your canvas looks similar to a page in an old black-and-white comic book. When you have finished, paint all the images out with a white paintbrush.

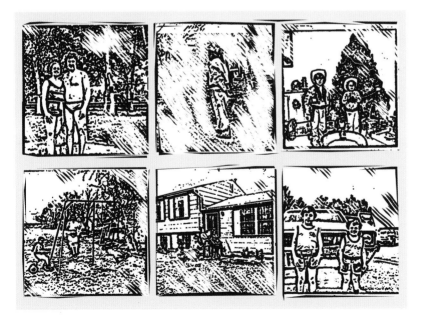

CREATING CONFIDENCE

Confidence gives us the faith to believe that we can achieve whatever we set out to do. We should be able to rely on ourselves, believe in ourselves, and believe in what we can achieve. This in turn will feed our self-esteem, self-respect, and self-control. Confidence tends to waver for everyone at times, so you need to know that you can bounce back after a setback.

When Balanced

- You have faith in yourself.
- You are loyal to others and not afraid to try new things.
- Your energy is channeled into what you want, whenever you want.
- You are not afraid to listen to and trust your instincts.

When Out of Balance

- You feel inadequate compared to those around you.
- You can have addictive tendencies.
- You feel yourself to be the victim in life.
- You believe that everyone else does better than you or has more than you.
- You can harbor feelings of jealousy or hostility toward others.

- You may feel suspicious of other people or even paranoid.
- You may feel intimidated by others' achievements.

Affirmations

- I believe in me.
- I need only my own approval.
- My achievements get better and better.
- I deal with everything well.
- I love new experiences.

Golden Moments

1. Find a quiet place, sit, and close your eyes.
2. Take a couple of deep breaths and relax.
3. Think of the things you have accomplished from childhood to adulthood: learned to ride a bike, learned to swim, passed exams, learned to drive.
4. Visualize yourself imprinting a picture of the golden moment on the pages of a large book.
5. Think of one or two more of these achievements.
6. Record them in the book.
7. When you have finished, close the book.
8. Put the book in a safe place for future use.
9. When you are ready, open your eyes.

After this meditation, it is a good idea to begin a real scrap-book of your achievements. You can then visualize the pages when you repeat this meditation.

Give Yourself a Boost

1. Find a quiet place to take a few moments for yourself.
2. Relax and take a few deep breaths.
3. Think of a person to whom you feel inferior, and visualize the person as larger than you.
4. See the person standing next to you, painted in a vibrant color.
5. Feel yourself grow to become the same size as the other person.

6. Picture yourself now made up of the same vibrant colors.
7. See the other person disappear.

SELF-ESTEEM

We are all born with a natural tendency to like and accept ourselves, which means that as children, we are open with our feelings and actions. Ideally we should continue this pattern as adults. Constant criticism can give us feelings of inadequacy, however, especially if they are endured over a long period. Even when nothing is said, feeling silent distain from others can be just as damaging to our self-esteem.

When Balanced

- You treat yourself with care and respect.
- You do not blame yourself for every mishap that happens in your life; you accept that bad things can happen.
- You see yourself as a competent, together person and realize your limitations.

When Out of Balance

- You listen to the put-downs of others and take them to heart.
- You may feel you have let someone down by not meeting his or her high expectations.

- You let others control you or you try to control others.
- You feel inadequate next to a sibling or close friend who is a higher achiever or a favorite.
- You feel worthless.
- You cannot forgive yourself for your past mistakes.

Affirmations

- I value everything about me.
- I deserve respect and happiness.
- I am unique.
- I am free to be me.
- I am worth it.

When Facing a Potentially Difficult Day

1. As you begin your day, sit on the edge of the bed.
2. Stretch your arms and take a couple of deep breaths.
3. Visualize a round golden shield.
4. See it covering your navel and abdomen.
5. Notice that the shield's surface is reflective; nothing can penetrate it.
6. Visualize it staying in place all day.

If you are laboring under excessive criticism, try the following exercise. While the person is criticizing you,

1. Turn your head so that the person is speaking into only one ear.

2. Lower your eyes and picture the person's words going in one ear, through your head, and out the other ear.

3. Take your focus away from the words and just watch the flow of energy moving into, through, and back out of your mind.

4. Drain all of the energy out of your head when the criticizing person has gone.

Rebuilding Your Self-Worth

1. Find a quiet place where you will not be disturbed.

2. Relax, close your eyes, and take a few deep breaths.

3. Take your focus to your third eye.

4. Visualize a circle filled with purple mist.

5. Step through the center of the circle.

6. See yourself on a path on a bright, sunny day. Stay on it as it meanders through a lovely garden, leading you to a pool.

7. Sit and look at your reflection.

8. As you do so, tell yourself the good qualities about yourself.

9. Tell yourself all the things you have achieved recently.

10. Congratulate yourself.

11. Leave the pool and take the path back through the garden.

12. Step back through the purple mist.

13. When you are ready, open your eyes.

LOVE OTHERS AND LOVE YOURSELF

How we give, show, and accept love from others affects all of our relationships, as does—just as importantly—the love and care we give to ourselves. Love boosts our morale, our ability to cope with dilemmas, and our ability to hope.

When Balanced

- You are honest in love and honest with your feelings.
- You feel that others are genuine and honest with you.
- You can laugh and cry naturally, not holding back your feelings.
- You are happy giving love and don't expect great things in return.
- You accept and love others for who they are, not who you would like them to be.

When Out of Balance

- You cannot move on from hurts.
- You feel unworthy to be loved by anybody.
- You harbor fears of loneliness or betrayal or both.
- You automatically push your own needs to the background.
- You are stingy with others or you deny yourself simple treats and joys in life.

- You can be dishonest in relationships and dishonest with yourself.
- You have a constant need to change others rather than accept them for who they are.

Affirmations

- I love who I am.
- I am attractive to others.
- It is easy to love me.
- Love is all around me.
- Love is always flowing through my life.

When you are sorting out matters of love, if you can find the underlying truth about what has happened, you are free to improve the situation or move on.

Focusing on Yourself

1. Find a quiet moment and relax.
2. Take a few deep breaths, and close your eyes.
3. Focus on a relationship in which you are feeling unbalanced.
4. Look at your part in the relationship.
5. Ask yourself what your feelings are.
6. Delve down to your real feelings and reasons for your unhappiness or feelings of irritation.
7. Be honest with yourself.

Focusing on the Other Person

1. Take a few deep breaths.
2. Focus on a relationship in which you are feeling unbalanced.
3. Look at the other person.
4. Determine whether the other person has expressed his or her feelings.
5. Decide whether what the person says matches what he or she does.

Deep Meditation: What Makes You Happy?

This meditation can be very effective if you record it over a favorite piece of music. It will have a strong effect if you practice it morning and night for a week or two.

1. Relax, take a few deep breaths, and close your eyes.
2. Take your focus down to the middle of your chest.
3. Open a golden door and follow a golden corridor to a place that you love.
4. When you get there, find someone with whom you have a special bond waiting for you there.
5. Talk with that person about what really makes you happy.
6. Discuss desires you have that are heartfelt and the thoughts that make you happy.
7. Talk about the things that interest and fulfill you.
8. Agree to meet again.
9. Return along the corridor and through the door.
10. Close the door and open your eyes.

COMMUNICATION

We communicate with others in many ways—by what we say, what we do, our facial expressions, and our body language. By the way we talk, we show what we feel, what we agree with, and whether we accept or like whomever we are talking to. The world communicates back to us, not only through speech but also through our other sensory organs, such as the eyes, ears, and nose. We need to communicate clearly with others and we need to know how to express ourselves. Poor communication can lead to misunderstandings, and being afraid to communicate can leave us isolated and lonely.

When Balanced

- You speak and think clearly and communicate in a non-threatening way.
- You see your mistakes and can formulate solutions.
- You are happy to listen to others as well as to speak.
- Your sincerity is apparent and you say what you mean.
- Your senses are alert and sharp.

When Out of Balance

- You may see only what you want to see or hear only what you want to hear.
- You may gossip.
- You may say one thing and do another.
- You scheme and manipulate others through your speech.

- You have a tendency to burst out with wild statements.
- You are too picky or fault finding.
- You hold back from speaking up for yourself.
- You fail to express your emotions or opinions when asked.

Affirmations

- I love expressing myself.
- I always speak what I feel.
- I speak my truth.
- It is safe for me to speak my feelings.
- What I say is worth hearing.
- My voice is heard.

A Humming Meditation

Humming and singing are good for clearing the voice. Talking and singing loudly help you develop confidence in your ability to speak up. So if you have swallowed what you have wanted to say recently, try this meditation.

1. When you have some time to yourself, hum one tone, emphasizing the *mmm* sound in your throat.
2. Change the tone, but again emphasize the *mmm* sound.
3. Practice *oms*, elongating the *mmm* sound and feeling it in your throat.
4. Play a song or piece of music and hum each note.
5. Now focus on building volume as you are humming.
6. Now sing a song you know well—loudly!

If you are frightened of saying what you want or what you feel in a situation, try this meditation.

1. Relax, take a few deep breaths, and lengthen your exhalations.
2. Lower or close your eyes.
3. Visualize yourself in the situation, facing the person who frightens you.
4. See yourself saying ridiculous things; they may be truths or utter nonsense.
5. Say things that you would never really say.
6. Continue until you find it too humorous to continue.
7. Now visualize the person's reaction.
8. Next imagine them saying silly things to you.
9. Think about whether what you are holding back is still so daunting.
10. When you are ready, open your eyes.

GIVE YOURSELF MOTIVATION

There are times when our sources of inspiration dry up, and there also are occasions when even the most wonderful career loses its allure and we find ourselves bored or frustrated. The solution is probably to look around for a new job, or at least for a fresh project, but sometimes that is not immediately possible, so you need something to help you keep going in the meantime. The following affirmations will help you tap into some initiative and find some balance until you can find a new direction.

When Balanced

- You are happy, inspired, and motivated; you have a healthy interest in your path through life and a drive to progress.
- You are moving forward in life.
- Your goals are realistic and you stick to them.

When Out of Balance

- You go around in circles.
- You find it hard to move forward.
- You have a tendency to start things but never finish them.
- You feel disillusioned.
- You find it hard to raise enthusiasm and you lose interest in things easily.

Affirmations

- There is much of life to explore.
- I am free to move forward.
- Today I will change my life.
- I am open to new directions.
- Happiness lies in new ideas.

To Help You Find a New Direction

Choose a favorite piece of music that you have found to be inspiring and play it.

1. As the music begins, relax with a few deep breaths.
2. Close your eyes.
3. Clear your mind and just listen to the music.
4. Feel the melody taking you forward.
5. Visualize two golden doors opening.
6. Go through the doors onto a brighter path forward.
7. When the music finishes, slowly open your eyes and align with the here and now.

Then . . .

1. Sit quietly, relax, and close your eyes.
2. Examine the main areas of your life.
3. Look at your work. Is it what you want?
4. Then think about your home. Are you where you want to be?
5. Next evaluate your relationships. Are you happy in them?
6. Think about whether you can create ways to move forward in all these areas of your life.

7. Visualize where you would like to be in one year's time.

8. Picture where you would like to be in five years' time.

9. When you have formulated your aims, open your eyes.

Begin a notebook of plans for your work, home, and relationships, and note down ways in which all these areas of your life can move forward.

THE REAL YOU

It is calming, strengthening, and inspiring when we let ourselves be who we really are. Some people believe that life is a journey that is designed to allow us to discover our true selves. Whatever you believe, when you are happy and feel good about yourself, it follows that you can create a fulfilled and happy life. You will look "alive" and you will know what makes you happy.

When Balanced

- Your clothes, hairstyle, and home suit who you are.
- You allow yourself to be creative in the way you dress.
- You know and accept what makes you happy and strive to incorporate this into your lifestyle.
- You understand how to pace yourself with work and projects, and you know your limitations.

When Out of Balance

- You feel lost.
- You set your sights too low when aiming for goals.
- You find yourself living by someone else's rules.
- You give yourself little attention.

Affirmations

- I enjoy discovering me.
- I look and dress who I am.
- I am moving forward.
- I love my creative side
- I am creative with myself.
- I strive to make myself happy.

To Attract a Better Future

Imagine that all restrictions have gone from your life, for instance, shortage of money, responsibilities, and commitments to anything or anyone. With this in view, follow this meditation, and as far as you can, visualize it in detail.

1. Relax, take a few deep breaths, and close your eyes.
2. Take your focus to your third eye.
3. Visualize a spinning circular disc, growing larger.
4. Walk through the center of the disc.
5. Visualize yourself redecorating your bedroom.
6. Imagine that you are getting new furniture.
7. Think about how it will look . . .

8. Imagine that your closet is empty.

9. Think about what clothes you will fill it with.

10. Blend with the spinning circular disc of light of your third eye.

11. When you are ready, open your eyes.

Now . . .

1. Relax, take a few deep breaths, close your eyes.

2. Take your focus to your third eye.

3. Visualize a spinning circular disc, growing larger.

4. Walk through the center of the disc.

5. Imagine that you are given the chance to embark on an interesting journey. Ask yourself: To which country would it be? What would you like to see and experience?

6. Visualize yourself making that journey.

7. When you have finished the journey, return.
8. Blend with the spinning white light of your third eye.
9. When you are ready, open your eyes.

Again . . .

1. Relax, take a few deep breaths, and close your eyes.
2. Take your focus to your third eye.
3. Visualize a spinning circular disc, growing larger.
4. Walk through the center of the disc. You are invited to a social occasion where you meet someone you have admired from afar. You have the chance to talk to this person.
5. Ask yourself: What would you want to talk to this person about? Why does this person interest or inspire you?
6. You are asked what you feel is your goal or mission in life. What do you reply?
7. See yourself blending with the spinning white light of your third eye.
8. When you are ready, open your eyes.

LET YOURSELF LIVE

Life is to be lived, experienced, and enjoyed. Fun, happiness, and new experiences should be consistent throughout your life, and it is up to you to make sure they are! We are all con- stantly growing, both mentally and emotionally, and as we grow so our lives move forward. If we stunt our growth, then in turn our lives become stunted.

When Balanced

- You see life as an adventure with new opportunities.
- You take charge and work toward making yourself happy.
- You decide whom to allow into your life, how much you are involved with them, and how much of your time they will share.
- You decide what or who will affect you and your actions.

When Out of Balance

- Your life is all work and no play.
- You resort to analyzing situations too much.
- You find it hard to let go and enjoy yourself.
- You feel a constant wanting or waiting for something.
- Your life is at a standstill.
- You could harbor a strong fear of dying or a fear of living.
- You limit yourself or see life as limited.

Affirmations

- I am unique and happy.
- I am growing and transforming my life.
- I am creating a new future.
- I am allowing fun into every day.

- This is the first day of the rest of my life.
- Today I am changing my life.

Change One Thing

1. Relax, take a few long breaths, and close your eyes.
2. Visualize yourself holding a clear crystal sphere in which you can see an aspect of your life (work, friends, home, money, chores, children).
3. In the aspect of your life that you have chosen, think about what you can do to take one step forward.
4. When you feel you have an answer, open your eyes.
5. Write down your answer in a notebook or somewhere else you can refer to for inspiration.

The Adventure

1. Relax, take a few long breaths, and close your eyes.
2. Take yourself back to when you were a child.
3. By inventing an experience or using a memory, go on an adventure of discovery.
4. Ask yourself: Which part of the adventure did you enjoy? Which part did you want to return to?
5. Now look at your life. Ask yourself: What parts nourish you and make you happy?

If you find this meditation difficult, try making a scrapbook of images that you find inspiring and focus on one picture for the meditation.

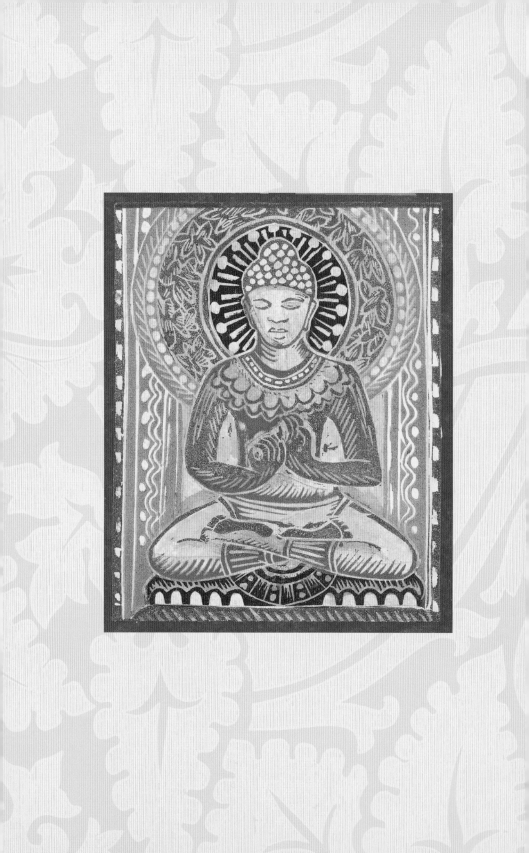

7

COLOR HEALING

There are many energies buzzing around our planet that touch us every day, such as electrical energy, nuclear energy, and the energies associated with gravity and the weather. Every living being gives out energy, as do some things that we may not have thought would do so, such as rocks, crystals, and colors. In addition, our thoughts and feelings create energy. Happy thoughts and feelings are good for our health, while negative ones create energies that make us feel bad. When we balance our thoughts and feelings, the energy in our bodies can change and heal us.

In the 1970s, scientists studied some of the trained meditation experts of the East and discovered that the mind has a powerful effect on the body. They also discovered that the human nervous system affects the body's immune system. Emotional and psychological stress can weaken the body's defenses against illness, but it has been found that visualizing colors can help you regain your energy balance and they can have a strong healing effect.

USING HEALING COLORS

Color is composed of light of varying wavelengths or frequencies that create an energy or vibration. Different colors vibrate at different frequencies, releasing different types of energy. For example, the energy of blue is calming and cooling, and the energy of red is warming and invigorating. Meditating on certain colors can link us to their energy, which can help us to heal and balance certain aspects of our bodies and our lives.

A simple way of meditating with color is to collect colored cards or papers (those with pure hues, which are sold in arts and crafts shops, are best). Pick a color that you are drawn to, sit quietly, and just look at the color for several minutes until you feel ready to stop. You can use colored bulbs to light the area in which you meditate to enhance the meditation. If you find yourself feeling low or overemotional, think back and see whether you have been wearing many dark colors over recent weeks. The color of your bedding and the colors around you in your home can also have an effect on you.

There are three colors that are regarded as powerful healers—green, orange, and blue; they are known as "universal healing colors." Each creates a healing effect or vibration, and each works in a different way, so let us now start with the color green.

GREEN

Green is nature's healing and growth color. As nature is balanced, so the color green can help you balance your life, helping you gain a clear perspective. Physically, green offers healing to nervous disorders, an overactive thyroid, and high blood pressure. Blood circulates through the heart, so green is helpful for arteries, veins, and major organs in the body such as the liver.

This particular meditation takes your emotional calendar back in time, so that you can rediscover the person you were before the layers of hurt and fear built up.

1. Sit in a quiet place and relax with a few deep breaths, making your exhalations longer than your inhalations.
2. Close your eyes and focus on a white beam of light shining down.
3. Picture yourself in the center of a white spotlight.
4. The white light turns emerald green; let it enter your body through the back of your heart center.
5. Let it fill the heart area of your body with emerald green.
6. Send out a stream of green energy from your heart area to a part of your body that you feel needs healing.
7. Allow the green energy to wrap around the organ or area.
8. Visualize that part of your body turning green.
9. Leave the energy there.
10. Repeat this process with a second organ, body part, or area.
11. When you have finished, leave the energy in your heart.
12. Close the back of your heart area by closing an imaginary door.
13. Send the spotlight of light up into the sky.
14. When you are ready, open your eyes.

You can repeat this meditation, using pink instead of green. A pale pink to a medium shade of pink soothes emotional hurts. It is good for releasing feelings of neglect or anger triggered by emotional betrayal or disappointments. To inspire a stronger sense of love for others, use a deep pink in the heart area.

Note: Green is not suitable for healing tumors or cancer, as it encourages growth. Red is good for these illnesses, as it burns out cancer cells, heals diseases of the blood, heals wounds, and also helps with depression.

ORANGE

Orange is the color of emotional healing, and it can be effective on a deep level. Focusing on the color orange in meditation can ease emotional trauma or an old hurt that you find difficult to let go. Orange can also help with bereavement. It is a good color for building up the immune system and rehabilitating your body after an illness. It increases motivation and sexual energy. Orange can also help with pneumonia, multiple sclerosis, the reproductive system, and the kidneys.

To help you address any of these problems, try this meditation.

1. Find yourself a relaxing, quiet place to sit.
2. Close your eyes and breath deeply.
3. Focus on making your exhalations longer than your inhalations, as this will help you to calm fraught feelings.
4. Take your focus down to the base of your spine,

and visualize a white spiral of light growing down from the base of your backbone.

5. See the spiral growing downward into the Earth, going deeper and deeper, until it reaches the orange glow of the Earth's center.

6. At this point see the light changing from white to orange.

7. Pull the orange energy up the spiral cord of light and into the base of your back.

8. Feel the orange energy flow into the lower part of your backbone and rise up to just below your waist.

9. From your backbone, feel the orange glow radiating forward, filling your abdomen, until this area of your body is full of the orange energy.

10. Feel this warm, gentle energy soothe you for several minutes.

11. Let the energy clear from your abdomen back into your backbone.

12. Then see it drain back down the spiral cord of light, returning to the Earth's center.

13. Pull the spiral cord of light up through the Earth and back into your backbone.

14. When you are ready, open your eyes.

Note: Too much use of orange can antagonize mental distress. Use orange sparingly if there are mental issues involved such as low self-esteem or a temporary loss of confidence.

BLUE

When babies are born, they are in touch with their spiritual selves, which is partly why they carry light blue in their aura or energy field. Blue calms the thoughts, soothes the emotions, and eases physical troubles. It reduces agitation and has a cooling effect that acts as a sedative for the body. In spiritual terms, blue is an "antiseptic" color that helps to strengthen the immune system.

Blue is physically useful for underactive thyroids, fevers, burns, nausea, and sore throats.

To access the blue healing color, try this meditation.

1. Find a quiet, peaceful place, and close your eyes.
2. Take some relaxing breaths, inhaling deeply and exhaling slowly, until you feel relaxed.
3. Take your focus to the center of your forehead, to the area that we call the third eye.
4. Visualize a white, spinning disc that grows larger and larger.
5. Watch as it grows large enough for you to step through.
6. See the white disc turning a vibrant royal blue.
7. As you walk toward the disc, see that it is made up of blue mist.
8. Walk into the mist and feel it enter the front of you and sweep right through you, turning you royal blue.
9. See your skin, hair, muscles, and bones turn blue.

10. As you step out of the mist, feel it leave the back of you.
11. Turn and walk through the mist a second time; let the color sweeping through you again.
12. Allow it to blend with your body.
13. When you are ready, open your eyes.

COLOR AS A PURIFIER

Meditating on certain colors sweeping through your body can be like washing your system on the inside, then energizing it. Imagine the following colors as mists that you walk through, or as a color that enters the top of your head, and which you then draw down your body on the inside from the top of your head to your feet. You can visualize parts of your body, such as your skeleton, organs, muscles, or skin, turning various colors as a method of healing.

WHITE

White is made up of all colors of the spectrum, and it is highly cleansing. It clears away stored negative energy in the mind, body, and spirit. It can amplify and strengthen healing if used at the beginning and end of a healing-color meditation. It purifies, eases conditions including physical pain, and gives spiritual calmness and comfort. Physically, white can help heal headaches and skin ailments as well as depression and exhaustion, and it can help those who have epilepsy.

For healing with white light, please see Key Meditation 2: The "White Light" Meditation on page 12.

Using white light to heal another person can be very effective, and other colors can be used to supplement it. When doing this, ask your friend or client to sit in a chair. You stand behind the chair. Place your hands on your client's shoulders and visualize white light coming down into the top of your head, down through your head, along your shoulders, down your arms, and out of your palms. Allow the light to flow into your client, moving your hands if you feel you want to. If you would like to use another color after white, let it come through your head and onto your client. Follow your intuition to decide what colors to use and when to stop.

SILVER

Silver works as a purifier in the same way as white, but it can break down areas of debris in the energy field (the aura). Silver can speed up your vibration, helping you achieve better concentration while meditating. This color triggers inspiration for creative projects such as art, music, and writing, so it can be useful to meditate on if you have a creative block.

It is beneficial to perform the white meditation before the silver meditation. Follow these steps to perform the silver meditation.

1. Sit in a quiet place, relax, and close your eyes.
2. Take your focus to your third eye.

3. Visualize your reflection in a round mirror.

4. Around your body see a ring of energy.

5. Take note of any gray or dark areas.

6. Fill the ring of energy with silver.

7. Watch the gray or dark areas melt away as the silver filters through them.

8. Now see the silver color begin to penetrate your skin.

9. Visualize stepping into the mirror and blending with your image.

10. When you feel satisfied that you have blended with your reflection, step back out of the mirror.

11. Take one final look in the mirror and see your energy field turning to gold.

12. Visualize the mirror again becoming a white spinning disc.

13. Take your focus down to just below the center of your rib cage.

14. When you are ready, open your eyes.

GOLD

Gold has been highly regarded since ancient times, when people believed it to be sunshine that had solidified into solid metal. It has a very fine frequency of energy that puts us in touch with our surroundings. It is the best color to repel or disperse negative energy. It is the most uplifting color for lightening heavy moods, but it should be used gradually at first because of its strong vibration.

Follow the steps below to perform a gold meditation.

1. Sit quietly, relax, and close your eyes.
2. Take one or two deep breaths.
3. Send up a thought for a golden shaft of light to come from a high point in the sky.
4. As it reaches you, see it turn into hundreds of raindrops showering through you and your energy field.
5. Feel negative energy washing away from you and into the ground.
6. When you have finished, send the light back.
7. Open your eyes.

TURQUOISE

Turquoise can provide emotional or physical healing, but I suggest that you use it as a form of psychic protection. So, after using the gold, silver, and white meditations, visualize yourself putting on a vibrant turquoise cloak with a large hood that falls over and covers your forehead. Fasten the front of the cloak so that your body is covered. You can put on two, three, or more cloaks, one on top of another, until you feel thoroughly protected. Alternatively, you could imagine yourself getting into a turquoise sleeping bag and zipping it up all around you.

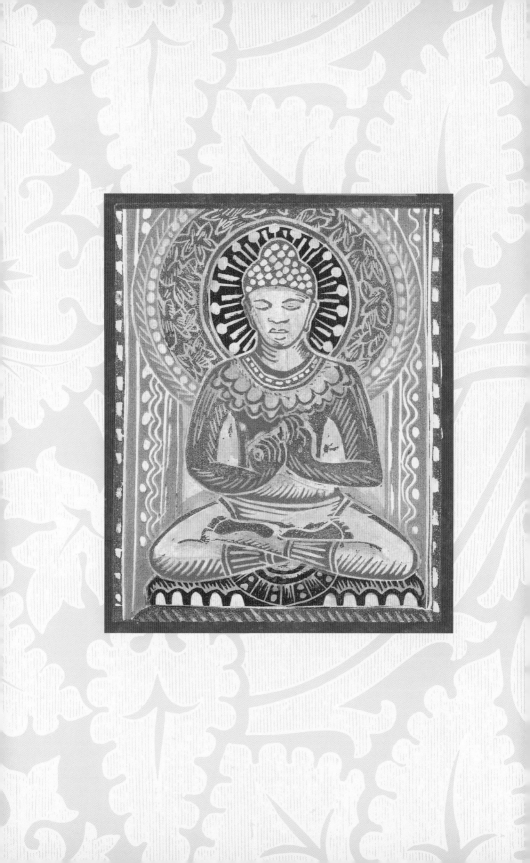

8

NATURE'S HEALING

The countryside and lovely landscapes have a calm, untouched, nonchaotic energy that allows you to still your thoughts and emotions. The color green is abundant in nature, and as this is the color of your heart center, it can restore you to your natural self or give you self-awareness. Nature is straightforward and uncomplicated, yet always busy creating and growing. People relax outdoors but also see nature as a source of inspiration, with activities such as rock climbing, hiking, and sailing. In these days, it is often good just to breathe some fresh air.

Beautiful natural scenes of landscapes and waterscapes can have a calming and healing effect, and birds and animals can help heal and empower you. When using nature for meditation, make the meditation more effective by focusing on an ideal natural place. If you can, actually go to a favorite spot and focus on the scene, try to absorb as much detail as you can, so you have a strong memory that you can tap into later for meditation purposes.

EARTH

The Earth contains a very creative energy. Plants grow from the Earth, and water springs from beneath rocks. The Earth absorbs negative energy, which it is able to change from negative to positive. We see this in the cycle of nature as things grow, mature, grow old, and die and sink back into the ground, from which new life springs from the nutrients.

Earth Meditation 1

1. Visualize your feet buried in the earth up to your ankles.
2. Feel the earth energy being pulled up through the arches in your feet, then through your legs and into your abdomen.
3. Allow the earth energy to bring you spiritual strength and endurance.
4. Once you have drawn the strength you need, allow the earth energy to trickle back down into the Earth once again.

Earth Meditation 2

1. Visualize yourself on a camel riding across the golden sands of a desert.
2. Feel the warmth of the sun as you approach a settlement.
3. See brightly colored tents stretched out in front of you.
4. As the desert sand ends, jump down, feeling warm, soft earth under your bare feet.

5. Lead your camel to drink fresh water.
6. Lie down in the large bathing pools of shallow mud and cover your whole body in warm, soft, purifying mud.
7. Feel negative energy being drawn out through your skin and absorbed by the mud.
8. Wash the mud off under a gentle waterfall.
9. Remount the camel and set off across the desert once again in the sunshine.

WATER

Water is an emotional healer, and visualizations of any type of natural water source, for instance, waterfalls, lakes, or the sea, are useful.

This water meditation works on a deep, emotional, healing level, helping you clear away old hurts, distresses, and anxieties. It is useful when you find it difficult to move on from an emotionally harrowing situation. Practicing this meditation can help you to heal and strengthen.

1. Sit quietly and focus on deep breathing, this time making your inhalations longer than your exhalations.
2. Close your eyes and take your focus to your third eye.
3. Open a white camera shutter and move through it.
4. Visualize yourself standing at the foot of a gentle waterfall, and hear the sound of water running down the rocks.
5. Notice a pool gathering at the foot of the waterfall.
6. Step toward the pool and put your bare feet in the water.
7. Visualize two camera shutters opening in the soles of your feet, and draw the water right up your body to the top of your head.
8. When you are completely full of water, let the water drain back out through your feet, taking any negativity, hurt, or unhappiness with it.
9. Close the camera shutters in the soles of your feet.
10. Step out of the pool.
11. Feel yourself blend back into your body.
12. When you are ready, open your eyes.

MOUNTAINS

Mountains are seen as still, strong, solid, and immobile. This meditation is ideal if you feel you are being carried along by fast-moving events. Perhaps you feel uncertain of yourself or feel that you need to step back from a situation and reassess it. Alternatively, you may feel that you have spent too long trying to achieve something and you are losing faith.

1. Find a quiet place to either sit or stand.
2. Focus on your favorite hill or mountain, or imagine your own beautiful, large, soaring mountain.
3. Imagine that you are outside on a bright, sunny day, standing on a path leading you to your mountain.
4. Picture yourself growing as large as the mountain.
5. Absorb yourself into the mountain and feel the strong, still base, the large, circular width, and the strength with which it supports its own weight.
6. Imagine the timeless stillness of a mountain being formed many thousands of years ago and remaining for thousands of years to come.
7. Allow the strength and stillness to be absorbed into your being.
8. Feel that you are calm and strong.
9. As you feel yourself become the mountain, allow your eyes to look out from the pinnacle and feel your vision take in views from all around.

10. See clearly all that is taking place for miles.
11. Give yourself the time to observe all that is occurring.
12. Remain strong and steady with your progress.
13. Feel yourself come out of the mountain and return to normal size.
14. Walk back along the path and in through the spinning light into your third eye.
15. When you feel centered in your body, open your eyes.

TREES

Trees are seen as a form of energy or life. You will make this meditation more effective by actually doing it in a forest. If this isn't practical, go to a park where there are trees or to a wooded area, and absorb the scene into your mind's eye for use when you have the peace and time to meditate on it. Vary the experience from time to time: visit the wood at different times of year and at different times of day, as the energy of early morning is very different from that of evening, and springtime will feel different from winter. This is a long meditation, so you might want to record it and then follow the recording for your meditation.

1. Complete Key Meditation 1: The "Grounding" Meditation, on page 10.
2. Take your focus to your third eye and visualize a white spinning disc.

3. Watch the disc growing larger and larger; when it is big enough, step through it.

4. See stretched out in front of you a sunny country scene with trees, hedgerows, grassy fields, and a path.

5. Begin to walk along a path that meanders into very pretty woodland, with shafts of sunlight falling through the trees.

6. As you walk through the woodland, see old and new trees and wildflowers.

7. Come across a clearing and walk into the center, where there is a large old tree with a thick trunk.

8. Sit, leaning back on the tree, and relax.

9. As you look around, be aware of the time of day and the season.

10. Focus on the sounds you hear in the forest.

11. Ask yourself: What do you smell?

12. Ask yourself: What do you taste?

13. Ask yourself: What do you see around you?

14. Ask yourself: Is the air warm and still, or is a gentle breeze blowing across your face?

15. Put your hands on the ground.

16. Think about what you are touching.

17. Your feet are bare. Think about what you feel under them.

18. Put your hands on the bark of the tree. Feel the texture.

19. Take your focus now to the tree. Begin to blend in with it; feel yourself extend down into the deep roots, pulling up food, water, and the natural earth energy.

20. Now rise up the trunk, feeling yourself stretching into the branches.

21. Feel the solid strength of the tree, the stillness of the tree, and the sunlight being absorbed into the leaves.

22. Look out at the forest from the top of the tree, as the tree would view the forest.

23. Feel yourself now coming down from the high branches and up from the roots, shrinking to your normal size inside the tree.

24. Now come out of the tree and imagine yourself once again sitting and leaning against the trunk.

25. Connect again with being on the ground of the forest, viewing the woodland from your normal sight level.

26. When you are ready, stand up and make your way out of the clearing, back onto the path, and out of the forest.

27. Now return back in through your third eye and back into yourself.

28. When you are ready, open your eyes.

POWER ANIMALS

Power animals are used in shamanism, which itself is the world's oldest healing practice. Shamanic elements can be found in all cultures, particularly in healing meditations or the meditation journeys made by the Native American tribes and the ancient Celtic peoples of Britain, Northern Europe, Russia, and Scandinavia.

The shaman, or medicine man, works with power animals to heal. When meditating with power animals, you go on a visualized journey, either as the animal or with the animal, to experience a natural way of being, because animals and birds are not complicated themselves and they do not complicate their lives. We may lose natural ways of surviving hardships, but by meditating on power animals we can pick up on their positive energy. Power animals are always wild creatures—anything from insects and reptiles to sea creatures and mammals. They help give direction and purpose to life. They free you from the assumption that you are a helpless victim of circumstance or that fate controls your life. Meditation with power animals connects you with nature so that you can discover who you are and what your purpose is in this life.

When using power animals for a healing meditation, you may wish to imagine the animal as it would look soon after birth, then using your mind's eye, watch it grow into a mature animal. The same goes for birds, whereby you can start by imagining an egg, then a tiny bird, a fledgling, and later a full-grown bird. This is not quite so easy to do when meditating on insects, but butterflies emerge from a chrysalis and other insects start off small and then grow larger.

The Bear

Bears are thought to know the planet as a living being, and Native American and other traditions say that bears can connect us to the heartbeat of Mother Earth. Their energy protects us from harm and from negative energy given out by others in the same way that a parent protects a child. Bears are also associated with knowledge and understanding of dreams and daydreams. By using either polar bears or brown bears in meditation, we can create protection for ourselves from the negative energy of others. Mothers give their children teddy bears, and although this tradition is only around one hundred years old, the bear is an ancient symbol of nighttime protection.

The Brown Bear

Brown bears hibernate and spend much of their time asleep, so a brown bear meditation can help dispel fears of the dark or of being alone. This kind of meditation helps us to heal our inner child, which is the core or child in us that our adult traits are based on. Brown bears live in caves, which are believed to represent the womb of Mother Earth. They symbolize a link with rocks and minerals found in caves and with healing crystals.

The Polar Bear

In a meditation, a polar bear is believed to provide a healing and nurturing influence that protects you when your family has failed you. These loving and protective bears can help you feel that you are a part of the world. Wonderfully fluid when they swim, polar bears are connected to the element of water and thus to all types of emotional healing. They can survive in very barren, cold landscapes, so their energy can help you to survive loneliness and separation.

The Wolf

In a meditation, a wolf is connected to the idea of protection when you venture into new places, either as part of a group or on your own. The wolf is swift, alert, and strong, and it can be a pack animal or a loner. It has powerful instincts and a talent for survival.

The Deer

The healing aspect of the deer is the idea of mending difficult situations by helping you to calm down and listen to others. Deer excel at watching and listening because they are alert and wary. They have sharp instincts, they can smell danger, and they are associated with the concept of clairvoyance. Unless disturbed, they live in the present, in a gentle, peaceful, and graceful way that is in complete harmony with their surroundings.

The Frog

The frog image in a meditation offers healing and cleansing to the emotions and feelings; therefore, it aids you when you are suffering from worry, stress, and nervousness. Frogs live in the "emotional" element of water and are very flexible and adaptable, so their energy can be used to help you become less rigid with your emotions. Frogs start life as eggs, and then become tadpoles and eventually frogs, so meditate on being the tadpole, then see yourself grow into the frog; this process will symbolically help your character to develop and grow stronger.

BIRDS AND INSECTS

Birds in shamanic healing are seen to be balancing as they fly, using two wings of equal size on either side of their bodies. They fly high and observe the world from an elevated viewpoint, which offers them a clear picture. They are also spiritually and intuitively strengthening.

The Eagle

The eagle is the highflier among birds and is considered the most spiritual, so it connects you to guides and helpers in the spirit worlds. The eagle can take you way above this world and strengthen your spirit. This large bird brings strength, courage, and wisdom and rises above the material world of money and possessions. The eagle sees the bigger picture of what life is all about.

The Raven

Meditate on the raven when you need healing or after an upsetting or traumatic situation, as a raven meditation can help remove fear. The raven is able to find light in the darkness; therefore, it guides you when you feel lost. The raven endows you with the strength to change or tear down what needs to be rebuilt in your life; thus, it can help you get over a bad relationship or find a decent job after time spent in the wrong line of work. It also can help you overcome unhealthy or addictive habits.

The Owl

The owl can transform your thoughts and feelings from low and bad to good and happy. The owl is silent and swift and can see behind the masks that people put up to hide their real selves. An owl meditation can help you to discover anything that others are keeping from you that could harm you, while also helping you to keep your own private life to yourself. The owl can improve your powers of insight when your vision in a situation is cloudy. You can meditate on an owl to solve a problem, but it's best to focus on only one problem with each owl meditation. Even though owls can turn their heads in a full circle, seeing all around them, dealing with more than one situation at a time will complicate matters.

The Swan

Swans are believed to understand love and heart-to-heart contacts, so swan meditations are helpful when you want to heal hurts that arise from partners and relationships. Swans transform from ugly cygnets to large, graceful, beautiful birds that mate for life. Swans live on water, and psychics consider water the "feeling" or "emotional" element, so this makes swans sensitive to emotions. Swans can show you how to attract your physical partner. Meditate on yourself as though you were an adult swan, meeting with your swan mate.

The Hummingbird

This little bird is symbolic of joy and happiness, so a meditation on the hummingbird heals painful love situations. When you meditate on this bird, visualize a ray of healing light coming from its mouth.

The Butterfly

A butterfly meditation can heal shock and trauma, helping you to face things you have never faced before and to create a new beginning if you need one. Butterflies are always moving, constantly active, so their energy is transforming, changing weak thoughts and feelings into strong ones. Butterflies bring change for the better. In ancient Greece the butterfly symbolized a free soul. Butterflies can represent

great change and a positive outcome after you have been taken to the brink of disaster. They are seen as bringers of magic because of their metamorphosis from a slow, crawling creature to a beautiful flying insect. They inspire solutions that come in unexpected ways.

USING POWER CREATURES FOR PROTECTION

You can use the energies of any power animal for protection by visualizing your chosen animal as a kind of cloak around you. The head becomes your head, the animal's front legs or wings become your arms, and the animal's body becomes your body. If you do this several times, or with several animal images, you will feel a protective layer of energy developing around you. In shamanic beliefs, individuals should take on the energies of creatures that frighten them, such as spiders, snakes, and mice, because confronting these creatures in a meditation will heal them on many psychological levels. You could visualize yourself doing the positive things that they do, such as spinning webs, shedding shimmering skins, or running around a field.

9

A HEALING ROOM

The healing room meditation enables you to create an inner "healing room" or place that you can return to in your mind whenever you want to. Although the meditation represents a complete healing cycle, you can build on or add your own very personal healing by putting a picture, photo, or special object on a table or shelf nearby while you meditate. The meditation is designed to strengthen your intuition by exercising your psychic senses as well as clearing your system of suppressed negative energy. This will give you deep emotional healing and recharge your energy levels.

This meditation takes approximately thirty-five minutes and has a sequence of healing methods. You will gain the maximum benefit by recording this meditation on tape.

Note: You can do this meditation sitting or lying down.

Note: To receive the full benefit of this meditation, first complete Key Meditation 1: The "Grounding" Meditation and Key Meditation 2: The "White Light" Meditation, found on pages 10 and 12, respectively.

THE HEALING ROOM MEDITATION

1. Take several deep breaths until you feel relaxed.
2. Focus on your third eye and visualize a white spinning disc.
3. Watch as the disc grows larger and larger; when it is large enough, step through the center.

4. Find yourself in a white corridor.
5. See in front of you three steps and a white door at the top.
6. Walk forward, climb the three steps, open the door, and go inside.
7. Notice that you have entered a large white room.
8. Picture the walls being lined with shelves from floor to ceiling, with everything to make you feel better and heal you, such as medicines, herbs, books, and music.
9. See the large wicker baskets on your left.
10. Scoop up a handful of flower petals from a wicker basket on the floor and breathe in their aroma.
11. Then let the petals fall back through your fingertips into the basket.
12. Notice that on some of the shelves are brightly colored bottles.
13. Take a bottle of whichever color you are drawn to from the shelf, remove the lid, and smell or taste what is inside.
14. When you have finished, put the bottle back.
15. Notice that the back wall of the room is made up of a fine blue mist.
16. Walk into the mist and feel it enter the front of you and sweep right through you, turning you royal blue, inside and out.
17. As you step out of the mist, feel it draw itself out of your back.
18. Notice that the wall to your left-hand side is made of natural rock; hear the sound of water running down the rocks as a gentle waterfall.

19. See the pool gathering at the foot of the waterfall.
20. Step toward the pool and put your bare feet in the water.
21. Visualize opening two small apertures in the soles of your feet, drawing the water up into your body.
22. Feel the water rise up your body to the top of your head.
23. When you are full, allow the water to drain back out through your feet.
24. Step out of the pool and close the openings in the soles of your feet.
25. Continue to walk farther into the room, and then turn a corner.
26. See in front of you a huge stained-glass window through which sunlight is pouring, lighting up the room with pure shafts of color.
27. Under the window notice that there is a large carved chair.
28. Walk over and sit in the chair.
29. Arrange yourself comfortably in the chair, which is perfectly contoured to your body, stretching out your arms on the armrests.
30. Feel the sunlight soaking into the top of your head, your shoulders, your forearms, and your legs; then feel it through the whole of your body.
31. Feel the sunshine soaking into your skin and muscles and bone structure and energizing the very core of you.
32. When you are energized, get up out of the chair and make your way back.

33. Turn the corner toward the blue mist, passing the
    waterfall.

34. Once again walk through the blue mist.

35. Make your way back through the room toward the
    door.

36. Stop at the door and look back at the room.

37. Know that you can come to your own healing
    room whenever you feel you need to.

38. Know that you can add to the shelves anything personal that you use to make you feel better physically, mentally, or emotionally.
39. Now go through the door and leave the room.
40. Walk back down the steps and along the path.
41. Come back into your body.
42. When you are ready, open your eyes.

VISIT A HEALER

A meditation in which you visit a healer can be very effective if you have a strong belief in a particular healer, whether it is a healer who has actually treated you or a well-known healer whom you have read or heard about. If you are feeling fatigued or sad, focus your mind on the healer for a few minutes, imagining his or her eyes, and you will soon feel more energetic and happier. Alternatively, give yourself a full treatment as follows.

This meditation is most effective if you lie down or if you are in bed, just before you go to sleep. It's best not to direct the treatment in any way; just accept whatever you feel comes your way; it will be what you need.

1. Close your eyes, relax, and take your focus to your third eye.
2. Visualize a white spinning disc, growing larger and larger.
3. When it is large enough, step through the center.

4. Visualize yourself on your way to your chosen healer's practice.
5. Arrive at the door of the healer's office.
6. Enter and make your way to the waiting room.
7. Wait until you are called into the treatment room.
8. Visualize the room as you walk in and greet the healer.
9. Lie on the couch and visualize the healer beginning the treatment.
10. Allow yourself to relax, and you will feel energies at work.
11. When you feel the healing has finished, thank the healer.
12. Make your way out of the building.
13. Return through the light of your third eye.
14. Blend in with your body.

Note: If you fall asleep while you are having the treatment, don't worry—you won't do yourself any damage. As soon as you wake up, complete Key Meditation 1: The "Grounding" Meditation. If you regularly practice this meditation, you will feel something different happening each time, as the healing changes according to your needs.

10

PSYCHIC ADVANCEMENT

Everyone is naturally psychic, and we all have psychic experiences—a gut feeling, a premonition, a feeling of déjà vu—practically every day. In addition, we all read the thoughts of others to some degree, and many people experience occasional out-of-body sensations and give themselves some form of healing.

If you think back to when you were a child, you may remember knowing certain things without having been told anything about them. You may have felt spirit people around you or you may have had vivid, incredible dreams. Psychic ability springs from our natural instincts and is a natural extension of our intuition. If we choose to disregard our natural intuition, it will remain dormant, but if we pay attention to it, our psychic abilities will increase.

Psychic information comes from our physical senses of touch, hearing, sight, smell, and taste. These senses not only experience the physical world around us; they can work together to become a *sixth sense* or a *psychic sense*. When we pick up information psychically, we experience that information it in a multisensory manner—we see, hear, feel, smell, and taste things beyond our immediate surroundings. Our senses work by reading energies, including those forces that surround people and those that create atmospheres. This psychism can also include "seeing" future happenings.

The happier and more relaxed you are, the faster you will progress in your psychic development. Meditation is an intrinsic part of refining your psychic skills, and it can help you lift your vibration; the higher your vibration, the happier you feel.

CLAIRSENTIENCE

Clairsentience, or "clear feeling," is a sense that nearly all of us are aware of. It can range from a gut feeling or a sense of danger to a strong sensation or to just *knowing* something. It is the impression you get when you meet someone for the first time, and the sense people often have of walking into a room and feeling uneasy. When you develop this sense, you can expand it so that you can pick up on things that are wrong, sometimes in great detail. Clairsentience is more common in emotionally based people than in logical people, and it is more common among women and children than among men.

The following isn't so much a meditation as a way of opening yourself to the atmospheres that your and other people's energies create.

Focus on feeling what the energy is like around you, and wherever you are, try to feel the energy or atmosphere of the place. Try to sense the different energies in different places, such as shops, different streets, the doctor's office, or the various rooms of your home. Do the same in natural surroundings such as the countryside, your yard, a park, a forest, or the seaside. This is easy to practice; simply try to sense the energy of where you are.

Examine the effect that nature has by sensing what the energy is like in early morning, at midday, in the late afternoon, at dusk, and at night. Let yourself be aware of the feelings that different types of music generate. Tune in to the feelings that various people emit and those that animals give you. Finally, gauge the different feelings that your own thoughts evoke.

CLAIRVOYANCE

Clairvoyance is French for "clear seeing," and this process goes a step further than just seeing the solid world around us. It is a matter of receiving information in the mind's eye or the third eye in the form of images or symbols that represent situations and feelings. Some clairvoyants see images of animals from the spirit world or the auras around living things. Some see things exactly as they are, while others see things in the form of symbols. Many clairvoyants use both techniques. A typical symbol a clairvoyant might see is a ring when someone is getting engaged, or a crib when a baby is coming. These are well-known symbols. Other clairvoyant images, such as archetypes, need interpretation. Archetypes are original and ancient symbols that our ancestors would understand, for example, a jester, which could mean fun and laughter or entertainment; a wise old woman, which could symbolize ancient knowledge; or a sword, which could predict trouble or fighting. The theory is that some part of our memory is inherited from our ancestors; therefore, we can often understand these images, and their meaning is known universally.

Symbols can also be very personal to each individual, as they come from each person's subconscious mind. You could ask someone how he or she is feeling, and then clairvoyantly "see" an image of your bed. You know that it is daytime and that the only time you take to your bed during the day is when you are ill. Then the person tells you he or she has been ill. You can meet someone new and suddenly get a passing flash of an image of someone else; this tells you that the new person is like the one whose image you picked up. You may see objects or situations in your life, such as a part of your house, and then discover that this person is altering the same part of his or her house.

A particular symbol can mean something different to each person. For instance, for one person a bar of chocolate shows something that they have given up eating, but another would see it as a source of energy or a source of pleasure. Symbols are not fixed with one meaning; you have to interpret each image based on how you feel about it.

The following is a light meditation that will help you to develop your clairvoyance.

1. Picture a scene you enjoy, such as a lovely sandy beach, a woodland, or country walk.
2. Focus on seeing as much detail as possible, including the leaves on the trees, blades of grass, and grains of sand.
3. Open up your other senses: imagine what sounds you would hear and natural elements you would feel, such as a cool breeze.
4. Touch things and imagine their texture.
5. Ask yourself: What smells and tastes would you find there?
6. Focus on the point between your eyebrows where your third eye is located.
7. Visualize a closed camera shutter, and open it.
8. Inside is another closed camera shutter; open this one as well.
9. Yet again there is another shutter inside; keep opening the shutters, layer after layer.
10. Or, use the image of a flower instead if you like; in this case, you would open the petals bit by bit.

If you practice this meditation, you will strengthen your ability to use clairvoyance accurately and be able to see images more clearly.

PSYCHIC HEARING— CLAIRAUDIENCE

Our sense of clairaudience, or "clear hearing," involves hearing impressions of sounds, words, voices, or music that are not audible to normal hearing. The sounds will seem to originate in your head or to one side of your head and slightly behind one ear. Sometimes you will get a clairvoyant image, such as an initial or letter, at the same time that you experience clairaudience.

The main proof you are using clairaudience is that you are hearing words that you would not normally use or that you would not otherwise know. You might hear these in your own voice or less commonly in the voice of another person. Clairaudient messages can come from the telepathic thoughts of others, where you may actually "hear" what the other person is thinking, although you will usually pick up fragments of sentences. It can also come from people who are now in the spirit world and who want to pass on messages, or it can come from a spirit guide. This is part of mediumship, which is also called channeling.

With clairaudience you can hear some things clearly, but at other times the sounds will be fuzzy and unclear, as if the dial is slightly off when tuning in to a radio station. All that may be picked up is the general sound of a word or an initial. You may be hearing the name Sheryl but you may only actually hear the *sh* sound, or a guide might be passing on the name Jamie and all you hear is the *ee* sound. Successful clairaudience is a matter of tuning in to the right frequencies.

Both physical sound and clairaudient sound vibrate at certain rates, so clairaudience is achieved by widening our ability to sense a range of certain frequencies.

The following light meditation will help you to make a start on clairaudience or improve on the gift you already have.

1. Focus on conjuring natural sounds in your head, such as wind through the trees, rain on the window, or a waterfall.
2. Concentrate on the sound of a crowded room, a train station, and different voices.
3. Focus on the sounds of music, various instruments, individual singers, and choirs.
4. Tune into more subtle sounds, like a fire burning, a clock ticking, or the sound of your breathing.

A Special Meditation for Clairaudience

1. Imagine a golden light around your head and ears.
2. Now imagine that you have a radio tuner inside your head.
3. Notice that, when you tune it in to certain stations, you can pick up different frequencies.
4. Take a few moments to tune in to the main station—the one that connects you to your psychic abilities—and notice that your hearing begins to subtly change and expand.
5. Now notice that there are further channels, one to connect you with the world of animals and plants,

another for telepathy with other people, one for messages from people in the spirit world, and one for spirit guides who can help and teach you.

6. Choose a channel and try to sense a fine sound.
7. Leave yourself open to any sound impressions that you may hear.
8. When you have finished, move the channel selector to a lower frequency and let your hearing adjust to normal hearing.
9. Try to avoid noisy, bustling places immediately after this meditation, because you will pick up unwanted psychic disturbances from the people crowding around you.

CLAIRALIENCE AND CLAIRAMBIENCE

Clairalience means "clear smelling," and clairambience denotes "clear tasting." This may sound far-fetched, but smelling things that aren't there is an extremely common form of psychic ability.

For example, you smell smoke, yet there is no fire or anybody around you smoking. These impressions are usually connected to the spirit world, often indicating that a spirit is near. These smells can vary from scents of flowers, perfumes, and cigarette smoke to smells of baking or tastes of food or certain drinks. Sometimes the past lingers, so that you enter a building and smell what used to be there, such as a smell of animals that used to be kept there. Alternatively, you may smell hay or manure. A musty smell might be a symbol of the age of a building and of the passage of time, while freshness indicates the future.

Sometimes when you are searching for a word of advice for someone, instead of words you may be given smells or tastes that have a symbolic meaning, such as "Wake up and smell the coffee." A smell or taste may jog your mind or bring a proverb to mind.

DEVELOPING YOUR PSYCHIC SMELL AND TASTE SENSES

Be aware of different smells and tastes everywhere you go, such as inside shops and markets, in other people's homes, on the street, in a town or city center, around different people, or outdoors. See whether you can detect smells that do not belong or that do not seem to be coming from any-thing physical. Then focus on the smells of objects such as things made of wood, metal, plastic, or liquid. Do clothes smell different from your furniture's upholstery? When you are away from these places and objects, try to imagine their smells. Focus on the way that foods and drinks taste, and remember the taste after you have finished eating or drinking. Can you conjure up the taste of your favorite food, or perhaps the bitter or sweet tastes, or different textures of the food?

Bring certain smells and tastes to mind and think about who or what you relate them to, such as whom a certain scent reminds you of. Write these connections down and familiarize yourself with these symbols, as this will help your use of psychic symbols.

CLAIRCOGNITION

Some people can receive information on a psychic level that acts as an aid to creativity. Indeed, there are some artists and musicians who believe that other artists and musicians who lived and died long ago can come forward and help them to become more creative. Others feel that they receive information from their spiritual guides.

11

MORE PSYCHIC MATTERS

TELEPATHY

The phone rings and you know who's on the other end of the line before you answer. That is telepathy, as is having the same idea at the same moment as another person. This is not so much a psychic power as a *telepathic link*. Thoughts possess their own energy, which can travel over great distances in an instant. The stronger the feelings behind the thought, the more impact it has. If someone is thinking of you with feelings of devoted love, anger, passion, or hatred, you may feel it.

We are all telepathic to some degree, receiving and transmitting information most of the time without being aware of it. Some of us are better at transmitting, while others are successful receivers. The thoughts you receive telepathically are often a mixture of images, feelings, or words or phrases that may link together to make sense.

STRENGTHENING YOUR TELEPATHIC SKILLS

Take a willing friend or someone you know well and sit opposite to him or her. Tell the person to relax, and then shut your eyes. Visualize that you are inside the other person's head and looking out of their eyes. See what impressions, images, feelings, and physical sensations you get. Tell the other person of anything that you receive. If you feel resistance and cannot engage with the person to look out of his or her eyes, do not persist. Your partner has put up a block, and you will not be able to overcome it. Instead, visualize yourself standing behind the person, within his or her energy field. Tell the person what you are receiving, but don't be discouraged if you are wrong while you're still new to this.

The following exercise shows you how to transmit thoughts. Enlist the help of a friend, and then take a few minutes to visualize your friend in a simple situation that can evoke feelings, such as walking in an icy wind, standing by a warm fire, floating in water, climbing a mountain, or flying. Ask your friend how he or she feels to see whether the sensations you have sent have been successfully transmitted. Keep experimenting and you will soon improve.

Note: Be careful of using telepathy to send thoughts to hurt or upset someone, as by doing so you lower your own psychic vibration and leave yourself open to unpleasant energies.

REMOTE VIEWING

Remote viewing or astral projection is a stronger form of telepathy. It involves taking your mind to a distant place and being able to see that place, to be there psychically, or to know what is happening there. Some believe that we can travel across time as well as distance and see events that happened a long time ago or even view parts of future events.

Many of us can astral project or travel to various locations on Earth, and some can apparently explore other planets and dimensions. Some people believe that we leave our bodies most nights when we are in the deepest part of our sleep, and travel around the planet or beyond. However, when you learn to view by remote means, it is best to begin by using a place that is familiar to you, and to move on to unfamiliar locations later. This process will take perseverance, as it takes time to master.

Work with a friend whose home you are familiar with. Ask your friend to go into the bedroom or into some other room where he or she is unlikely to be disturbed. Ask your friend to move or set up some items around the room or on the floor. Visualize yourself going into the house, entering by the main door, and making your way to the room where your friend is. As you proceed, try to see the details of the house as if you were physically there. When you reach the room where your friend is, try to see it as you remember it from previous visits; then scan for impressions of the things that your friend has placed there. Check with your friend to see how accurate you are. After you have had some practice at this task, ask your friend to place an object in a box or container; then see whether you can find the container, describe it, and say what is inside.

CONNECTING WITH YOUR SPIRIT SELF AND THE SPIRIT WORLD

The spirit world exists on a higher level than ours, and spirit energy has a faster vibration than ours. When spirit beings communicate with us, they slow their vibration down, and we in turn need to speed ours up so our energies can match and meet on the same level. To speed up your vibration so that you can receive information and messages is very simple. The calmer and happier you are, the higher your energy vibration rises. You need to open energy centers or chakras, because these are your psychic and spiritual centers. By grounding yourself, opening up, and using white light, you can lift your vibration and rid yourself of surplus negative energy.

OPENING YOUR CHAKRAS

Root (or Base) Chakra

Some people call the first chakra the root chakra; others call it the base chakra. It is located about three-quarters of an inch (two centimeters) forward from the base of your spine. It is the slowest-spinning chakra, and it creates the color crimson as it spins. Visualize this chakra as a closed red flower, and focus on it opening; then, once the petals are fully open, imagine a round clear space in the center of the flower. Then imagine white light spinning in this center.

Sacral Chakra

Move up to the center of your abdomen, about two inches (five centimeters) under your navel. This is the location of your sacral chakra. This chakra spins slightly faster than the root chakra, creating the color orange. Open the petals of the orange flower, and open the center of the flower, revealing a round, clear space. Spin the clear space or center with white light.

Solar Plexus Chakra

The solar plexus chakra is situated slightly above the naval. (Some people feel theirs toward the left of the navel.) This chakra spins faster than the sacral chakra and creates the color yellow. Open the yellow petals of the flower and the flower's center. Spin the clear center with white light.

Heart Chakra

Move up to the center of your chest to your heart chakra, which spins at a medium speed, creating the color emerald green. Open up your green flower, and clear the center of the flower. Spin the open center with white light.

Throat Chakra

Your throat chakra is situated at the lower end of your neck. This chakra spins at a fast rate of vibration and creates a vibrant sky blue. Open up the blue flower, and clear the center, allowing it to spin with white light.

Brow Chakra, or Third Eye

Your brow chakra, or third eye, is positioned between and slightly above your eyebrows, and it is colored indigo. Open the indigo flower, clear the center, fill it with white light, and spin the white light.

Crown Chakra

Now move to the crown of your head and your crown, or seventh, chakra. This chakra is visualized as either white or pale lilac. Open the petals, then the flower center, and clear it. Then fill it with white light, and spin the light.

USING A LIGHT BODY

A very effective way to connect to the spirit world is to wear what is called a "light body." The strongest of these are the shamanic light bodies of power animals, such as an eagle, snow-white owl, hawk, brown or polar bear, wolf, raven, or crow. If you don't know which type to use, it is best to take yourself through a meditation in which you try different light bodies to find which one you feel comfortable with. If you wish, you can wear up to three different light bodies at a time, or even three of the same type. For further information on animals, review Chapter 8, "Nature's Healing."

Once you have opened up your chakras visualize yourself receiving a beautiful crystal robe in the shape of a bird or an animal. If you have decided to use an eagle, visualize the feathers as crystal, or if you are using an animal, then see the fur as crystal fibers. If you decide to use an eagle, visualize the crystal head of the eagle sitting over your head, and for a couple of seconds focus on looking out of the eagle's eyes and imagine you are this strong, alert, highflying bird. Your arms become the wings, and the back of the bird becomes your back. Your legs and feet become those of the eagle, and the bird's underbody closes around the front of your body. Sweep light from the bottom of your feet to the top of your head, lifting and lighting the feathers.

Now you can ask to work with your highest guides, which are of absolute light. Ask them three times to come and work with you. Ask for the room's energies to be cleared and the will of God, the Great Spirit, the Universe, or the Source to be done.

Now you are ready to practice any of the meditations that follow in this chapter, until you have finished meditating, when you must complete the closing sequence.

THE CLOSING SEQUENCE

At the end of a meditation or spiritual working session, it is important to close your chakras, or you will be leaving yourself too open and will feel vulnerable to everyone's negative energy.

Take your attention to your crown chakra, dim the light, and slow down the spinning. Close the open center of the flower petals. Then follow the same sequence, moving down to your third eye, then your throat, then your heart, solar plexus, sacral or abdomen chakra, and root or base chakra. Visualize the "light body" lifting from your shoulders, and send it up into the shaft of white light. You can simply open your eyes or you can put on some energy protection.

ENERGY PROTECTION

This is a worthwhile thing to do at the end of meditating when you have closed your chakras. This will prevent you from feeling supersensitive to atmospheres and to the negative emotions of others. An effective energy protection is to use colored cloaks. Powerful healing and protecting colors to use are gold, silver, or the three universal healing colors of blue, orange, and green.

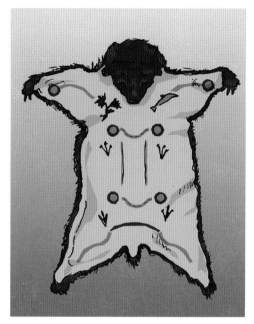

1. First, choose the color you like or need.
2. Feel a cloak in your chosen color come down from above in a tube of light, until it falls over your shoulders and fastens at the base of your neck over the center of your throat.
3. Close the cloak over your body chakras and bring a large hood up over your head, with the front falling over your third eye.
4. Keep putting on cloaks, one atop the other, until you feel that there is a layer of protection around you.
5. Be aware that it is useful to make the final cloak brown or to turn the surface of the final cloak brown, as this is a good color for mental clarity and grounding.
6. Consider also using shamanic animal robes as robes of energy protection.

Other forms of protection involve imagining shamanic drums sitting over the solar plexus and abdomen. This form of protection bounces negative energy straight back to those who are sending it. Negative energy includes insults, anger, aggression, criticism, and abuse. A mirror can be used over the solar plexus, or a full-mirrored suit of armor, complete with helmet and visor, body suit, gloves, and boots, can be worn if you are venturing into very difficult situations. The energy bounces back very quickly, and it can even make people aware of how badly they are behaving. It's worth remembering that if you don't rise to these people when they make remarks, the negative energy immediately returns to the sender.

THE UNIVERSAL HEALING PLANE

The universal healing plane allows you to give healing to yourself and others. Start by completing Key Meditation 3: The "Spinning Disc" Meditation, on page 14. Next complete the steps of the following meditation.

1. See in front of you a white stairway leading upward.
2. Climb up a set of thirty steps and cross a landing.
3. Climb up a short set of five steps across the landing.
4. Climb up a set of seven steps across that landing.
5. At the top see a doorway leading into a large crystal hall.
6. Walk in and make your way through the hall.
7. See the large crystal precipices that project over a pure-water stream.
8. Sit on the edge and dip your feet into the cool running water.

9. Feel a strong white light flowing down through the crown of your head and through your body, pushing any negative energy out of your feet.
10. Watch the negative energy float away down the stream.
11. When you are ready, stand and make your way back to the entrance.
12. Now see a straight stairway leading down.
13. Return to ground level and the hallway.
14. Leave the house and make your way back through the garden.
15. Then return through your third eye.
16. When you are ready, open your eyes.

12

MEDITATION AND RELIGION

Many religions encourage people to meditate for various purposes; for example, if you were to go to a Catholic retreat, you might be encouraged to meditate on your own life and on Christian images.

Following is a brief overview of some Eastern religions, along with a selection of their meditations.

BUDDHISM

Buddhism comes from the teachings of the Lord Buddha, and the word "Buddha" comes from Sanskrit and means "awakening." The main aim of Buddhism is to achieve spiritual enlightenment, thus enabling its followers to live a happier life. Unlike other religions, Buddhism deals with guidance through teaching, not with upholding traditions or revelations of truth.

The Buddha was the man who discovered and taught the path to enlightenment and happiness. He is seen as mortal, proving that it is possible for all human beings to achieve enlightenment, though it may take many lifetimes.

The dharma means "as it is" or "what is," and it refers to the teachings of Buddha. The dharma includes the Four Noble Truths; the Eightfold Path; dukkha, which means "inevitable suffering"; samsara, which is the cycle of birth, life, death, and rebirth; *anicca*, which shows that nothing lasts forever; and lastly karma, which is the chain of cause and effect.

Every moment that your mind is free of greed, hate, or delusion, the Buddhists believe a force develops called *parami*, which is a pure force of energy that builds within your mind. When you have a great accumulation of pure force, then the results are many kinds of happiness. There are two kinds of *parami*, or purity of mind, and this is shown in two ways: purity of actions and purity of wisdom.

Meditation is central to Buddhism, so there are many different kinds of meditation that serve a variety of purposes. Following is a lovely one that is designed to encourage you to develop a pleasing and friendly attitude.

The Metta Bhavan

1. Find a quiet place to sit and relax, and close your eyes.
2. Follow your breaths, counting beats for how long you can comfortably breathe out and how long you can comfortably breathe in.
3. Do this for a few minutes if you can.
4. Next, think of positive feelings that you have for yourself, focusing on pleasant aspects by silently making statements such as "I am happy" or "I am well." Alternatively, dwell on a memory of a time when you felt really happy, or wish yourself happiness and let the feeling grow.

5. Then think of someone you know in your life, such as a good friend.

6. Picture the person really happy, and wish him or her happiness.

7. Next choose a person that you do not know very well and for whom you have no strong like or dislike, such as a person you see in passing every day on the train or at work. Picture the person happy, and wish him or her happiness.

8. Next choose someone you do not like at all, someone who works against you or who has hurt or upset you in some way.

9. Try to see past the person's bad points and realize that he or she just wants to be happy.

10. Picture the person happy, and wish him or her happiness.

11. Now picture the friend, the neutral person, the enemy, and yourself all feeling the same good feelings, and then wish happiness for all four of you.

12. Next, widen your scope, think of others around you, picture them happy, and wish them happiness.

13. Then look beyond—to those who live in your area, in your town, in your state, in your country.

14. Think of all the people who live there, and feel and wish them well.

15. Wish them the same happiness that you wish yourself.

16. Then think of everyone in the world and all living creatures; picture them happy and wish them happiness.

Mantras

Mantras are words or phrases whose sound vibrations have a strong impact on the person saying them as well as on those who hear them. Each word has a sound pattern that reaches the mind with its meaning and acts as a trigger for the emotions. Mantras are regarded as power words and are used as a focus in Buddhist meditation. One such mantra is *Om mani padme hum*, which means "Jewel in the heart of the lotus." It is used for opening the heart center, allowing you to give love and kindness and to accept them from others. To use a mantra in a meditation, sit quietly and repeat the mantra either in your mind or out loud, focusing on the words and the sounds that they make. They are meant to be repeated many times, and for several minutes, preferably every day.

ZEN

In approximately AD 475, an Indian Buddhist teacher named Bodhidharma took Buddhist teachings to China. There the teachings spread, blended with Taoism, and became the Ch'an school of Buddhism. Seven hundred years later Ch'an Buddhism was introduced in Japan, where it is known as Zen Buddhism. It is the base of the martial art of karate, and also of archery and swordsmanship. Many people take up Zen meditation because it improves concentration in sports and athletics as well as study. The following is one form of Zen meditation.

This method uses breathing as the main focus to clear the mind; you breathe in and out, focusing deeply on the rise and fall of the abdomen, while observing the intake of cool air and the exhalation of warm air.

TAO

Tao focuses on developing a sense of unity of mind, body, and spirit. When this unity is achieved, we are able to achieve what we want and do good for ourselves and for others. Tao teaches you not to look at life with your rational mind so much, but to experience life more like an adventure and to follow what fascinates you. In a way, you look at life as if it is a fairy tale, letting go of agendas and just experiencing the ride. In Tao beliefs, happiness comes in phases or cycles: we go through good times, we go through bad times, and then we go through good times again. The phase we are presently in is often followed by its opposite, so that a hectic social phase may be followed by a phase of quiet where we become quite lonely; then the hectic social life picks up again.

Tao is a Chinese philosophy, the main part of which is that you aim to truly appreciate being here and enjoying life; otherwise, there is not much point in being here! It is not so much a religion as a way of being. Translated, the word "Tao" means "the way."

In Tao everything is made up of, or works through, two opposite forces—yin and yang. Yin and yang are in every aspect of life, and everything is made up of these two opposites. Yin is the passive side, feminine, cool, slow. Yang is energetic, masculine, hot, and fast. Following are some examples.

- Sun is yang; moon is yin.
- Light is yang; dark is yin.
- Summer is yang; winter is yin.
- Boy is yang; girl is yin.
- Busy is yang; quiet is yin.
- Success is yang; failure is yin.

Yin and yang are related to the five elemental forces that make up the core of our world. These five elemental forces are water, wood, fire, earth, and metal.

Water kick-starts life, making all things grow.

Wood represents the things that are here and growing.

Fire is the spark of life, igniting activity and excitement.

Earth is what holds everything in place.

Metal represents the tools we make from the earth.

conclusion

Introducing meditation into your life will help you feel happier and more at ease with yourself. It will aid you in coping with life and understanding its twists and turns. It will also assist you as you try to relax. If your blood pressure is high, meditation can help you lower it. Meditation can also facilitate your contact with the spiritual realms. Regular meditation can support you as you try to handle your life more effectively.

Once you have tried out some of the meditations in this book, you may wish to join others who meditate or take training in certain aspects of meditation. With the rapid spread of meditation in the Western world, organizations and centers have opened up in many towns and major cities. If you are interested in any of the specialized types of meditation, contact your local Buddhist, Kabala, Zen, or spiritualist center for meditations in spiritual and psychic development. Yoga classes also practice meditation, as do some Christian groups, though you will need to determine whether the spiritual beliefs appeal to you before taking this route.

Good luck with your journey with meditation. I hope you discover many new ways to happiness through it!

acknowledgments

I would like to thank Sasha Fenton for making this book possible.

I am grateful for my students, who allowed me to take them through so many meditations and who taught me so much.

I thank my wonderful teachers and inspirers, Ruth McAleese, Mosey, David Cousins, Maria Bowden, Doreen Virtue, and Sasha Fenton.

My thanks to my father, who was skeptical of just about everything except meditation and who taught me my first meditation as a young child.

Thanks upon thanks to my sweet "favorite Marge," who believed in me and was always there with never-ending support. May you smile down on us from your star.

A special thank-you to Kaeleigh for helping us conceptualize the illustrations.

index